This book is dedicated in memory of Vera Hansen—and to all life-long learners everywhere.

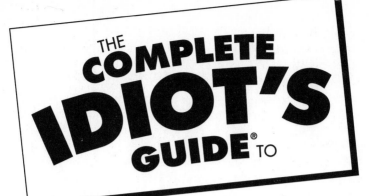

Study Skills

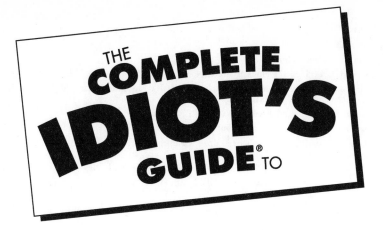

THE COMPLETE IDIOT'S GUIDE® TO

Study Skills

by Randall S. Hansen, Ph.D., and Katharine Hansen, Ph.D.

ALPHA

A member of Penguin Group (USA) Inc.

ALPHA BOOKS

Published by the Penguin Group

Penguin Group (USA) Inc., 375 Hudson Street, New York, New York 10014, USA

Penguin Group (Canada), 90 Eglinton Avenue East, Suite 700, Toronto, Ontario M4P 2Y3, Canada (a division of Pearson Penguin Canada Inc.)

Penguin Books Ltd., 80 Strand, London WC2R 0RL, England

Penguin Ireland, 25 St. Stephen's Green, Dublin 2, Ireland (a division of Penguin Books Ltd.)

Penguin Group (Australia), 250 Camberwell Road, Camberwell, Victoria 3124, Australia (a division of Pearson Australia Group Pty. Ltd.)

Penguin Books India Pvt. Ltd., 11 Community Centre, Panchsheel Park, New Delhi—110 017, India

Penguin Group (NZ), 67 Apollo Drive, Rosedale, North Shore, Auckland 1311, New Zealand (a division of Pearson New Zealand Ltd.)

Penguin Books (South Africa) (Pty.) Ltd., 24 Sturdee Avenue, Rosebank, Johannesburg 2196, South Africa

Penguin Books Ltd., Registered Offices: 80 Strand, London WC2R 0RL, England

Copyright © 2008 by Randall S. Hansen, Ph.D.

International Standard Book Number: 978-1-59257-799-6
Library of Congress Catalog Card Number: 2008922786

10 09 08   8 7 6 5 4 3 2 1

Interpretation of the printing code: The rightmost number of the first series of numbers is the year of the book's printing; the rightmost number of the second series of numbers is the number of the book's printing. For example, a printing code of 08-1 shows that the first printing occurred in 2008.

Printed in the United States of America

Publisher: *Marie Butler-Knight*
Editorial Director: *Mike Sanders*
Senior Managing Editor: *Billy Fields*
Executive Editor: *Randy Ladenheim-Gil*
Development Editor: *Julie Bess*
Production Editor: *Kayla Dugger*
Copy Editor: *Krista Hansing Editorial Services, Inc.*

Cartoonist: *Steve Barr*
Cover Designer: *Bill Thomas*
Book Designer: *Trina Wurst*
Indexer: *Heather McNeill*
Layout: *Ayanna Lacey*
Proofreader: *Mary Hunt*

Contents at a Glance

Appendixes

Contents

Introduction

We want this book to be your guide, your companion, to achieving greater academic success and achieving the success you desire—ideally, without your having to make great sacrifices or changes to do so.

Our agenda? Simply put, we want to help you succeed in school. We want to empower you to achieve the success you desire. We want you to view learning not as a struggle, but as a success. We want you to not only become a better student and develop an appreciation for learning, but also use these skills to move forward with your life and career beyond college. We'll help you break bad habits and establish new good ones.

We are both college professors, career experts, and parents. We know firsthand the academic struggles that some students face. We know that some school systems appear to do a poor job in preparing students for the rigors of college-level work. We know the pressures some parents put on their children to succeed—and the ensuing frustrations that come from not knowing how to achieve the success your parents desire from you.

We wrote this book to help you. We truly believe you'll be able to use many of the suggestions, tools, and tips in this book to perform at a higher academic level.

What's in It for Me?

Simply put, this book could change your life for the better. It might not seem as though grades are all that important, especially if you are a good student already. But believe us when we tell you that developing many of the habits and methods in this book now will also serve you well later in life.

This book can help you perform better academically. If you're struggling with grades, this book will help you pass your classes and feel confident about yourself. If you are doing average work, this book will help push you to higher levels of academic success. And even if you are currently a top student, you can learn still new things to improve your study habits and keep you achieving those top grades!

Besides doing obvious things like making you feel better about yourself, increasing your self-confidence and self-esteem, and making your family proud, achieving better grades will open more career doors (some employers screen applicants by grades) and help you gain entry to graduate school if you decide to continue your education.

Our goal is to help you become a strategic learner, a student who possesses effective and efficient study skills strategies for reading textbooks, taking class notes, studying for exams, and writing papers. More specifically, this book will help you become a better student by showing you how to ...

- Find the one best study method for you.
- Study more efficiently and effectively.
- Actively listen and learn.
- Manage your time and avoid procrastination.
- Prepare for classes and take better notes.
- Perform better on all types of tests.
- Conduct thorough research.
- Write well on everything from essays to term papers.
- Manage your stress and achieve balance.

Finally, this book will also help you be happier and more successful in general. You can easily apply many of the strategies in this book to life situations. You can use the time management or writing skills you'll develop (or the many other tips and tools you'll learn) to achieve personal and professional success.

How This Book Is Organized

This book is organized in five parts around something we call the TEST Method, a guide for developing solid study skills.

What does TEST stand for?

- Taking responsibility for learning
- Establishing success in the classroom

◆ Succeeding with writing

◆ Tackling tough issues

TEST is not some simple system for improving academic performance. It's a philosophy of becoming a better student that results in smarter study skills and higher performance in the classroom—a philosophy that you can incorporate into your life.

Part 1, "Pre-TEST—Laying the Groundwork," focuses on clearing your mind about academic success while preparing for success by examining study myths, rules for improving your grades, and study tips from top students.

Part 2, "Taking Responsibility for Learning," highlights the information you need to understand about yourself—and methods to improve any deficiencies—before you can achieve greater academic success. These include managing your time issues, finding your learning style, and reading strategies.

Part 3, "Establishing Success in the Classroom," stresses the tools you need to succeed in school, with special emphasis on four areas: class preparation and note taking, study tools, testing techniques, and special techniques for key subject areas.

Part 4, "Succeeding with Writing," spotlights the importance of writing in achieving academic success and covers such key issues as research methods, writing essentials, and success in specific types of writing assignments.

Part 5, "Tackling Tough Issues," gives you solutions to some common problems students face when they're attempting to improve their grades. We include ways to manage stress and achieve balance, as well as tips for times when your grades are not improving.

Extras

As you work your way through the book, you'll encounter some extra bits of information that we believe you will find helpful as you attempt to improve your study skills and achieve better grades.

Here's what you can expect:

Study Suggestions

Concise and useful tips and ideas for improving your grades.

Study Stories

Short anecdotes and inspiring words from real students who have achieved academic success.

Study Stressors

Activities, habits, and other things you'll want to avoid in order to improve your studying skills.

Acknowledgments

We've had some amazing students over the years—and not all of them were top academic performers. All truly valued learning and did their best to improve their academic performance. Many of these students are quoted throughout the book, graciously offering you, the reader, their wisdom and insights into academic achievement. This book is dedicated to all of our students.

Specifically, we would like to thank the following people for their enthusiastic input and support: Heather Albright, Emily Ball, Patrick Bauer, Steven Bennett, Laura Boyd, Jim Burleson, Cayla Culver, Peter Dzuba, Maria Forlivio, Stephanie Griggs, Matt Guy, Tracy Heidenfelder, Micaela Hermann, Jessica Hoch, Amber Janney, Erin Lovell, Megan McDonough, Ben Millar, Sabrina Otaibi, Sarah Petty, Marissa Pilson, Renee Poulin, Jill Sears, Morgan Seedarne, Jessica Walton, Laura Whalen, Adrianne Wilhelm, and Nicole Zarrella.

And a special thanks goes to our editor, Randy Ladenheim-Gil, for encouraging us to develop the best study skills book on the market—one based on our years of experience as college professors, solid educational research, and the advice of proven strategic learners.

Trademarks

All terms mentioned in this book that are known to be or are suspected of being trademarks or service marks have been appropriately capitalized. Alpha Books and Penguin Group (USA) Inc. cannot attest to the accuracy of this information. Use of a term in this book should not be regarded as affecting the validity of any trademark or service mark.

Part 1

Pre-TEST–Laying the Groundwork

Before you can truly begin using the TEST Method we discuss in depth in the other parts of this book, it's helpful for you to review these three chapters.

You'll find information on the most common study myths, rules for studying, and tips from top students. Once you've read these chapters, you'll have a strong foundation for understanding how to use the methods we discuss in the rest of the book.

Five Myths About Studying

In This Chapter

- ◆ Learn the truth behind common study misconceptions
- ◆ See the connection between studying and success
- ◆ Take a first step toward studying smarter
- ◆ Move beyond these five myths

Congratulations! By opening this book and reading this first chapter, you are starting the process of studying smarter and moving beyond some of the common misconceptions students often have about studying. Believing in these myths can actually block you from obtaining the academic success you desire.

If you're like the typical student, you may have breezed through high school on your way to college—or you may be in high school right now. But what you're probably discovering is that the study skills (if any) that might have worked for you in high school do not work for you in college. Of course, you may also be the type of student who has always had to work hard—maybe harder than you think you should—to get passing grades in high school, and for whom school is a constant battle.

For whatever reasons, many students have misconceptions about learning in school. Certain myths result in counterproductive, exhausting, and sometimes very bad study habits—all of which can result in weak academic performance.

This chapter is all about debunking the most common myths about studying to help you get started becoming a strategic learner, developing better overall study skills, and earning higher grades.

Studying More/Longer Results in Good Grades

Some people seem to think that the solution to getting better grades is simply committing more time to studying. In some ways, it would be nice if it were true. Then again, we should be happy it's not true: who wants to be stuck indoors all day staring at a computer screen or reading a textbook?

While it's true that you may need to commit more time to studying, preparing, reading, and writing, it is certainly not true that simply putting in more time will result in any kind of positive change.

Many of our students over the years have told us that they barely spent any time studying while they were in high school, so when they entered college, they assumed they needed to study longer to earn the grades they so easily had achieved in high school. Guess what? Just putting in the hours did not give them the results they sought. They had to find a better way.

We know a professor who has a chart that shows his students the grade they can expect based on how many

> **Study Stories**
>
> "It is strange, but I find that I am studying less now that I am in college—but I am studying the more important stuff. I have figured out which information is important in a textbook and which information is just a waste of space in my memory, and have adjusted my studying accordingly."
>
> —Emily B.

hours they study. How sad that he perpetuates the myth that studying more will result in better grades.

Using the tools and resources you'll find in later chapters of this book will help you develop an efficient study system that works for you. You'll still need to devote a lot of time to studying—but you'll learn that what matters most is not the number of hours you commit, rather the quality of studying.

Study Stories

"My first semester of college was kind of a wake-up call for me. I remember doing poorly on my first couple of exams and the pressure I felt from my folks to get the kind of grades I got in high school. So I doubled my efforts for the second round of tests and felt confident that all that extra time would improve my grades. Well, the midterms came and went, and so did my hopes for doing well in college. I was lost about what more I could do to improve my grades."

—Steve B.

There's One Study System Everyone Can Use

If you Google "study skills," you'll find a lot of people and organizations trying to sell you the one study system that will help you achieve amazing academic success. Maybe you already believe this myth because others have told you so. Maybe you thought this book was going to provide you with the "one" method.

Study Stories

"One thing I learned was that I had to adapt or change my study method according to the class. I couldn't study for a religion class the same way I studied for a finance class. But making sure I had enough time to study for each class—even if it meant carrying a planner with me at all times—was a big part of my success."

—Sarah P.

Unfortunately for all the unsuspecting buyers of these "proven study systems," no one system works for all students. Instead (and this philosophy is the premise of this book) each student has to discover the best system, partly based on issues such as personal learning style, available time, and reading and writing abilities. What worked for your mom, dad, or sister—or what works for your roommate—will not necessarily work for you. Furthermore, what works in one subject may not even work in others.

The reality is that studying—and finding the study method that works for you and leads you to becoming a strategic learner—takes practice and involves some trial and error until you find what works best for you.

The focus of this book is to guide you to becoming a strategic learner. We'll help you discover the most important aspects of academic success. We'll also guide you in developing a study system that consists of an inventory of study strategies that will help you achieve all your academic goals.

Knowing the Course Material Is Enough

One of the recurring themes of this book is the importance of knowing—really knowing—what is required of you in every course you take. Read the course syllabus very carefully and ask the professor about any areas of it that you don't understand. There's no excuse for not understanding what you need to do and learning if it is clearly addressed on the syllabus.

You might be asking yourself, "Aren't I graded on the course material, and thus shouldn't knowing it thoroughly be enough to earn the grades I seek?" Logically, the answer is yes, but that's the basis of this myth.

The truth is that college and college-level courses are designed to go much deeper than simple knowledge of the material. These courses are designed to make you apply the basic knowledge—terms, theories, and models—to new situations, to deepen your understanding of the topic.

Thus, while you certainly need to thoroughly understand the course materials, you'll often need to become much more proactive about your learning and find a way to deepen your level of understanding.

Study Stories _____

"I would describe my study method as proactive. I don't wait until I don't understand something or until I have a test to study. I stay on top of my work and start on projects soon after they are assigned. Each day I think about each of my classes and what is going on in them: what we are learning, what projects are in progress, and when the next tests are. If I didn't understand something from the day's lecture, I'll study it so that I don't get behind."

—Cayla C.

You'll find some great tools and suggestions later in this book for how to get to this deeper level of understanding that most professors seek from students.

Cramming the Night Before Will Keep Material Fresh

One of the common "urban legends" of college is that most students stay up the night before big tests and study in one concentrated effort. The story goes that if you study in this manner, the material will be fresh in your head and you'll be able to easily recall it for the test.

Study Stressors _____

Avoid cramming for an exam. As a last resort, it's better than nothing, but you'll accomplish very little of the detailed thought processes and analysis you get from studying daily. Plus, you'll face exhaustion because of the lack of sleep, have much higher levels of anxiety, and face higher chances of illness from a weakened immune system. If you do have to cram, focus your energies on basic terminology and lists that can be easily memorized.

The truth is that the best students do not—except out of sheer necessity at times—pull all-nighters. Instead, these high-performing students have learned the importance of studying over a longer period of time, actually learning and retaining the material rather than relying on short-term memory to perform well on tests and exams.

Study Stories

"I break up studying over several days and over the course of the evening and day. Cramming never works for me, so I try not to do it. I will have longer sessions on nights before big tests, but I never stay up much later than what is normal for me before tests. I know that if I take the test tired the next day, I will not do as well as if I was rested."

—Laura B.

This book will show you the power of long-term learning and the advantages of studying daily, which often results in fewer hours committed to studying—and certainly does away with the sleep deprivation and other problems associated with cramming and all-night study sessions.

Study Stories

"I recommend beginning to study for a test at least three nights in advance, because I have found that you don't actually learn when you cram the night before. And not only does that hurt your chances of doing well on the current exam, but it also means that, come finals time, you'll have to work twice as hard to study since you didn't learn the material the first time."

—Meghan M.

Writing Has Very Little Impact on Learning

We're guessing the person who started this myth was not very fond of writing because a vast amount of research shows just the opposite: writing has a very powerful impact on learning, retaining, and understanding course materials. Some researchers believe that writing helps students develop new knowledge—by sorting through previous understandings, drawing connections, and uncovering new ideas as they write.

Study Stories _____

> "I learned pretty early in college the power of writing stuff in helping me learn the material better. I would rewrite my class notes, take notes while reading the textbook, and even write my own study guides. I knew it helped me do better on tests, but it took longer to realize that not only was I remembering the material better over a longer period, but I was also able to begin making connections between classes."
> —Jill S.

The truth is, there is great validity to the idea that the more you write and rewrite your lecture and book notes, the more information you'll retain. You'll also be more likely to begin making the deeper types of connections and discoveries that are so important to academic success.

In terms of study skills and academic success, we'll show you in later chapters the value of writing and rewriting your classroom notes, writing reactions to textbook readings, and even writing study guides before major tests. Of course, we also devote several chapters to succeeding with written assignments, such as essays and term papers.

Study Stories _____

> "I rewrite my notes and form a study sheet for tests. This helps because not only am I *reading* it for at least the second time, I am also *writing* it for the second time. I have a photographic memory, so seeing my notes multiple times really helps me."
> —Amber J.

What You've Learned

Ready for a quick check to see what you've learned from this chapter? I now understand ...

- ◆ It's not necessarily the amount of time, but the quality of studying that results in better grades.

- ◆ I have to use the techniques discussed in this book and find the best study method for me.

- To achieve higher grades, I have to learn the course material at a deeper level than I may be accustomed to.

- Learning is a long-term process, not something that can be forced into a one-night cramming session.

- Writing can be a useful tool for all aspects of learning.

We'll spend the next two chapters further laying the groundwork for the TEST Method. First we look at five rules for improving your grades. Then we examine five study tips from top students.

The Least You Need to Know

- Achieving academic success in high school in no way guarantees that same level of success in college.

- Believing in some of the common myths and misconceptions about studying can actually result in lower grades.

- Becoming a better student means finding the study method that works best for you.

- Anyone can become a better student—a strategic learner—and achieve higher grades. Doing so will make you feel better and increase your self-esteem.

2

Five Rules for Improving Your Grades

In This Chapter

◆ Tackle important issues related to academic success

◆ Understand yourself and your motivations

◆ Learn five things you need for better grades

As we further lay the groundwork for the TEST Method, this chapter points out the five key things you need to do *before* you even start focusing on study skills to achieve better grades.

Don't skip ahead, thinking you don't need to read these rules. Everything else in the book will have little value to you if you don't first commit yourself to these five rules for improving your grades.

You may already follow some of these rules—and if so, all the better in terms of achieving greater academic success. Finally, some of these rules may be easier to follow than others, but do your best to change your behaviors to follow them. While you're at it, don't compare yourself to others; this is your journey to better grades—and yours alone.

What does academic success mean to you? We associate it with achieving a deeper level of learning, which, in turn, leads to better grades.

In an article in the *Journal of College Reading and Learning*, authors James Bell and Sara Short identified several ways that students defined achievement:

◆ Achievement is obtaining higher grades.

◆ Achievement is obtaining passing grades while balancing other factors (such as work and social life).

◆ Achievement is learning the course material (regardless of the final grade).

◆ Achievement is getting a passing grade—or better—on an extremely difficult course.

◆ Achievement is moving toward a chosen career goal.

◆ Achievement is avoiding certain negative behaviors.

◆ Achievement is growing as a person—into an adult.

You Must Want to Achieve Better Grades

Students face a lot of pressure to get good grades, and that pressure often begins way back in elementary school. Parents, family members, and teachers all tell you that you need good grades to advance to the next class level. Eventually, that message evolves to needing good grades to get into college. Finally, it transforms to needing to get good grades to get into graduate school or to get a good job.

Sadly, overbearing parents—mostly baby boomers—are a cause of academic weakness and failure rather than success. They've been labeled "helicopter parents" because of their

> **Study Stories**
>
> "You have to want to succeed, because no one else can make you successful. You are the one determining how much you'll achieve."
>
> —Stephanie G.

penchant to hover over their children and swoop down to come to their aid at the first sign of any kind of trouble. Experts say these overprotecting parents are actually hurting their children, not helping them. Students never learn how to cope with adversity, resulting in increased anxiety because they fear it implies that they are fragile and need continuous help to succeed.

Achieving good grades is tough enough without a parent constantly looking over your shoulder and questioning your every decision. How can you cope? Follow these strategies:

- Stop enabling your parents to control your life.

- Thank your parents for all their years of support.

- Show them you have a detailed plan to succeed.

- Enlist other family members to offer support for your plan.

- Provide a mentor or role model that you are emulating.

- Tell them that you want their support—but support of *your* plan.

So the first rule for improving your grades deals with *your* commitment to academic success. You have to take responsibility for your academic performance. You have to want to become a strategic learner, someone who possesses multiple study techniques leading to better academic performance. You are the person who is attending the classes, interacting with the professors, reading the textbooks, completing the assignments, and taking the tests. Thus, you are the one who has to ultimately make the decision that you want to achieve greater success. The reason you want to achieve greater success is not as important as the desire to actually do so.

Identify Your Study Strengths and Weaknesses

If you're the typical student, you've probably never done any kind of self-reflection or self-analysis on your study strengths and weaknesses.

Now's the time to conduct a realistic review of your study skills strengths and weaknesses. Think about your past academic successes and failures, classroom experiences, conversations with teachers, standardized test scores, and any other kind of feedback you've received. What stands out? Be honest with yourself; no one else has to see the results but you.

You should specifically examine your strengths and weaknesses in terms of time management, goal setting, note taking, focus/concentration abilities, anxiety control, reading comprehension, math abilities, test preparation, and writing skills.

Once you've had the time to reflect on this issue, the next step is putting your study strengths and weaknesses on paper. Grab a sheet of paper and put two columns on it. Mark one heading as strengths and the other as weaknesses. Write down what you consider to be your study skills strengths and weaknesses.

Study Suggestions

The best time to conduct your study strengths and weaknesses analysis is when you have an unlimited amount of time at your disposal. Also seek out a quiet and comfortable place where you can stretch out and really examine yourself and your academic experiences.

When conducting the assessment, be totally honest with yourself. Everyone has weaknesses; don't focus so much on them, but see this as an opportunity to turn your weaknesses into strengths. Once you've completed your assessment and composed your list of strengths and weaknesses, you'll have a much better handle on the areas of this book that you'll want to emphasize and focus on, to convert your weaknesses into strengths and make your strengths even stronger.

Studying Requires a Daily Commitment

The most successful students are the ones who long ago realized the importance of making a habit of studying daily. In the past, education may have been a passive experience that you sat through, but it's now time to take personal responsibility for your own learning—and to make a commitment to do so daily.

Study Stories _____

"I typically study or work on projects for a few hours each day—usually between or after classes. I like doing it during the day, partly because my brain is a little fresher then, but also because it then frees up my evening for fun stuff—social gatherings or just hanging out. I also do most of my reading for classes on the weekend, partly because those are days with no classes and big blocks of time, and partly so I can start the week having read all the material—and then just spend the days of the week reviewing my notes and such."

—Jill S.

Studying regularly in smaller chunks helps train your brain into thinking and retaining information differently, avoids the dreaded all-nighter to cram for an upcoming test or assignment, and gives you a more positive attitude about learning.

Here's a short daily study checklist:

❏ Have a goal for what you want to accomplish

❏ Complete all reading assignments

❏ Make sure you understand all the readings

❏ Finish all homework problems

❏ Start paper planning and writing early

❏ Review course calendars to check due dates

❏ Conduct mini reviews for your tougher classes

College students often have breaks of an hour or more between classes. These are the perfect times to study for an upcoming class or review your notes from a previous class.

We'll talk in later chapters about time management and organizational systems. For now, all that's required for you to find the time to study daily is your decision to do so.

Get Help Early and When You Need It

Too often students—even good students—wait until the last minute to request help. The longer you wait to seek help, the harder it will be to learn the material and the more likely your grades will suffer.

The time to seek help—from the professor, the teaching assistant, the academic success center, classmates, tutors, learning labs, or any other source—is as soon as you realize you have a problem. Don't be afraid to ask for the help you need, whether it's understanding a minor math formula or passing your Spanish midterm.

Speaking as professors, we suggest that your first contact for help be your professor or teaching assistant. Determine the professor's office hours and locate his or her office. Once there, explain how you're struggling and ask for suggestions for how you can improve. (See Chapter 15 for more tips on meeting with your professor.)

Study Stories

"A big thing that few students will do is to ask for help if you needed it. It's not a bad thing to not understand. It's a bad thing if you don't do anything about it."

—Laura B.

If you're too intimidated by your professor—or he or she was of no help—your next step should be on-campus clinics. Most schools offer math and writing tutoring labs, and many also have help rooms for a variety of other subjects. You may be able to find private tutors or even ask a classmate to assist you, too.

Set Reasonable and Achievable Goals

Setting goals for yourself to accomplish is an important activity because having goals can help motivate you to complete your studying, attend your classes, and strive to do your best on exams and other class assignments. Remember to also plan some sort of reward for yourself when you achieve your goal. (Yes, the grade is the reward for your hard work, but think of something else to reward yourself for your success.)

Here are some tips for goal setting. Each goal you set should state what you want to do, when you want to accomplish it, and how you'll make it happen. Your goals should ...

◆ **Be reasonable.** Stay within your skills and abilities.

◆ **Be realistic.** Don't shoot for an A if you have been earning C's.

◆ **Be measurable.** Don't just say your goal is to do better; be specific about what you want to accomplish.

◆ **Be believable.** You have to believe your goals are possible.

◆ **Be tangible.** Visualize yourself reaching your goals.

◆ **Be flexible.** Always be willing to modify as things happen.

◆ **Have a deadline.** Shorter time periods are better.

◆ **Be within your power.** Set goals only for things you control.

◆ **Have action steps.** Develop a plan to achieve your goals.

Some words of warning about goal setting are in order. Be careful about setting goals that are too much of a stretch for you. One of the best ways to set yourself up for failure is to set unrealistic goals for yourself. It's okay to push yourself with your goal setting—just don't push yourself over the edge. It helps to know your study strengths and weaknesses before you decide upon your goals. Finally, you should also be willing to regularly evaluate and revise your goals as needed.

Study Suggestions

All of these suggestions assume that your problems are academic in nature and not of some other variety. Of course, you should also seek help as early as possible if you have other problems, such as learning disabilities, health issues, or some form of addiction. If you're feeling stressed, see the suggestions for managing stress in Chapter 14.

> **Study Stories** _____
>
> "I never had any reasons to have goals in high school—other than going to college, which was just kind of expected. After a bad first semester at college, I realized I needed to improve my performance—and the way I did it was establishing some goals for the first time in my life, both for individual courses and for the entire semester of work."
>
> —Steve B.

What You've Learned

Ready for a quick check to see what you've learned from this chapter? I now understand ...

◆ It's my responsibility to want to achieve greater academic success and higher grades.

◆ I need to have a good idea of my study strengths and weaknesses so that I can make adjustments to my academic performance.

◆ To achieve higher grades, I have to commit to a daily study routine.

◆ If I am struggling for any reason, I should seek help as soon as possible to deal with the issue.

◆ Goal setting is a terrific way to achieve greater academic success—as long as I don't make my goals unrealistic.

We'll spend the next chapter further laying the groundwork for the TEST Method by examining five study tips from top students.

The Least You Need to Know

◆ Becoming a better student means following certain rules or guidelines.

◆ Some of these rules may be easier for you to follow than others, but to achieve great academic success, your goal should be to follow them all.

◆ Becoming a strategic learner and achieving academic success takes a personal commitment.

Chapter 3

Five Tips from Students

In This Chapter

- ◆ Find great study tips from top-performing students
- ◆ Get an insider's look into obtaining better grades
- ◆ Learn five tips for better grades

This book is full of advice from real students—high-performing academic achievers. But in this chapter, we focus on the five top pieces of advice these students offer to help you achieve the academic success you seek. You'll get a quick overview of each of these tips and then read actual quotes from students about the tips.

How you choose to use these tips is totally up to you. As college professors, we can attest that these five tips are all excellent pieces of advice. And we know from experience that the best students use these tips to their advantage.

Ready to learn some very easy things you can do to improve your academic performance? Just follow these five great tips.

Study in Small Chunks Instead of One Long Period

Just about every one of our top-performing students discussed this tip—the value of small but concentrated study periods followed by longer nonstudy periods. These students found they understood the materials better and retained more information longer by using this technique.

Studies show that planning your studying in small chunks, with breaks in between, is a much more effective way to learn material because the brain's concentration powers begin to fade after about 45 minutes. Breaking up your study time also helps you stay more actively involved and better organized—and each time you finish studying a chunk, you'll feel better because you'll have accomplished something.

Besides breaking up your studying into chunks, you should break up what you study. In other words (except for the night before an exam), study a mix of your subjects instead of focusing on just one of them.

Don't forget to take breaks—they serve two purposes. First, a break is a good time for the brain to absorb and digest what you've just studied. Second, it's always important to build in some rewards—even little ones—to treat yourself for your hard work.

Here's what our students have to say:

"I feel like I don't retain an adequate amount of information unless I actually give myself the time to absorb and understand the material. If you rush yourself, you'll feel more pressure and panic—and panic usually never results in good test scores." —Jessica W.

"I understand how I operate, and I know that I can't study for extended periods of time, so I break it up into smaller chunks and make sure that I do fun things and hang out with my friends in between, no matter how busy or stressed I am. It actually makes me more productive in the long run." —Erin L.

"My study method is usually an early morning one. My mind is fresh and ready to learn in the morning, and I usually don't have classes. I find that I do so much better if I get up early and study a little bit of each class every day. It is so important for me to review everything as I go along. It is impossible to do well if I cram it all in the last minute. I tried that strategy once—not good!" —Emily B.

> ### Study Stories
>
> "I know many people who break up their studying over several days, or even weeks, and I feel that is a great way to really learn the material and let it sink in. Being a collegiate athlete, however, I did not have the time to study all the subjects a little each night or each week. I still made good grades in college, and oftentimes studied the night before, or a couple nights before for a few hours each time. Looking back, I would have liked to study in small blocks. I feel like I could take a lot more from it, not just for tests, but to really learn the material."
>
> —Laura W.

"I usually have a few smaller blocks of studying. I find that this helps me to not feel overwhelmed and to keep my brain from blending everything together. Reviewing my notes helps me to prepare for the test and ensures that I'm not rereading everything for the first time on the night before the test. I set aside at least one hour a night to do homework, study, or prepare for projects." —Amber J.

"I have a lot of smaller study blocks throughout the week, and then I have one massive study block the night before the exam to make sure that I really know the material." —Marissa P.

"My overall study method is review, review, review. I have a difficult time retaining information when I study for long periods of time, so I try to break up my sessions into an hour of studying and 15 minutes of break." —Megan M.

When Possible, Review Previous Tests/ Assignments

If you can obtain some insider information—by reviewing previous tests and assignments—why would you not do so? Many teachers put previous tests, projects, and papers on reserve somewhere—in their offices, department offices, or the library. Some student groups also collect these items.

Our point here is not about cheating or copying old materials. It's more about looking for patterns of what is expected on these tests and assignments—and also how they are graded.

Reviewing previous tests is a great way to understand exactly the types of information the professor wants you to learn—and provides great insights into how you need to learn the material.

Here's what the chemistry department writes on a web page that contains about 50 old tests (along with the correct answers): "This is a collection of general chemistry exams from past semesters. They may or may not have been written by your instructor. The material covered in lab and lecture varies from semester to semester, so the old exams may not cover exactly the information your class has covered. These exams are, however, a good resource for you to evaluate your understanding of chemistry in preparation for your own exams."

Here's what our students have to say:

"When there is a big project due for a class, one of the first things I do is ask the professor if there are any good samples of previous projects that I could look at." —Steve B.

"My sorority keeps a file of major tests and papers from the last couple of years, and I take advantage of those as much as possible—especially at the beginning of a term when I really don't know what to expect from the class. And amazingly, some professors don't change their tests or assignments much from year to year." —Jill S.

Develop a System That Works for You

The best students realize that, just as no single study system works for everyone, their own systems sometimes need to change based on the type of class or professor. Strategic learners realize that, to succeed, they must be flexible in applying various study strategies to new situations.

Don't forget that you may need to change your study process midway through a course, especially if it is not working as effectively as you'd like. Don't ever be afraid to tinker with it—or even make a major change—if it will improve your grades. Remember, don't just increase your time commitment as a possible solution—consider other study methods.

This book is full of ideas and techniques designed to help you reach the academic success you seek. Throughout, you'll find a lot of study strategies. Your task is to develop a system that's successful, easy to manage, and keeps your stress to a minimum.

Here's what our students had to say:

"Find a strategy that works for you and stick with it! Everyone is different." —Emily B.

"I had to add study habits once I got to college because I never really had to study in high school. I had to make sure that I set aside time every night to do my homework and review my notes." —Amber J.

"Finding your rhythm is the key. Since my weekends are spent working, I tell myself that I will do all my assignments for next week during the current week. This can get difficult because it is hard to sit down and work on homework after sitting through three classes back to back." —Morgan S.

"It takes a while to find what method of studying works best for you." —Tracy H.

Learn What the Professor/Teacher Expects

This tip may be the most important—not just in this chapter, but for the entire book. One of the easiest ways to improve your grades is to determine exactly what your teacher or professor expects—and then do it! Sound simple? It is, and yet the vast majority of students never bother to do so. You can try to catch your professor before or after class, though most prefer you visit during their scheduled office hours (which are often listed on the course syllabus, along with the office location).

Study Stressors

If you decide to meet with your professor, don't whine and complain, bring along a parent, show up unexpectedly and demand time, or skip a planned appointment. And don't ever tell the professor—as we have heard one too many times—that you couldn't find him or her during scheduled office hours, especially if you showed up at a time when the professor didn't have office hours. (Find more tips in Chapter 15.)

Speaking again as professors, we can assure you that we would much rather receive all really great projects and assignments—ones that follow all our guidelines and are completed to our expectations. Yet that rarely happens. Many students take the time to ask their fellow students about the assignments—often gathering incorrect information—but seldom ask the professor to clarify what is wanted.

The other benefit of talking to your professor about your work, your progress, or an upcoming test or assignment is that just your presence in his or her office shows the professor that you are serious about your work. You'll also get valuable feedback on what the professor thinks of your work—and perhaps some tips on what you can do to improve. Finally, for larger classes in which you may have been an anonymous student, your visit helps the professor connect a name with a face. (Learn other benefits in Chapter 7.)

Study Suggestions

If you're an extremely shy person or a student in a megaclass who has no opportunity to talk with the professor, here's the best source to determine exactly what the professor is seeking in his or her assignments: the course syllabus. The syllabus not only lists the assignments for the semester, but it also provides details about what is included, how parts will be graded, and important due dates. Becoming an expert on the syllabus is also a step to becoming a strategic learner.

Here's what our students have to say:

"Make sure you understand what is being asked, and don't be afraid to ask if you don't understand. I had a history professor one semester who always had a section where you would have to explain the significance of key historical events or figures. He wasn't looking for a definition or an identification; he was looking for what impact that event or person had. I understood that, but many of my classmates didn't, and their test scores reflected it." —Stephanie G.

"Never be afraid to go ask your teacher for help. They have office hours for a reason; use them!" —Sarah P.

"Here's a cool thing I discovered (a little late in the game for me, but something that can help other students). If you listen—really listen—to your professors when they are lecturing, they will almost always give some strong hints on which material is the most important—and even how it might be asked about on the next test! One professor of mine would say something like, 'This is one of the top 10 concepts we're learning this semester.' Of course, I swear he used that line more than 10 times, but those concepts he mentioned were always focal points on his tests." —Jill S.

Using Brain Fitness Techniques

One of the coolest ideas we've gotten from our achieving students is the importance of a healthy body—the connection between being physically active and mentally active.

According to SharpBrains.com, "There are four essential pillars to maintaining a healthy brain that functions better now and lasts longer. Those pillars are: physical exercise, mental exercise, good nutrition, and stress management."

We focus on physical exercise and good nutrition in this section. If you're in school, you're completing mental exercise daily, so we'll skip this one since the whole book sort of deals with this issue. Finally, we'll cover stress management in Chapter 14.

A growing number of scientific studies show a connection between physical fitness and brain fitness. Exercising increases blood supply and sends oxygen to the brain, resulting in better memory, reasoning, and concentration; helps in the survival of current brain cells and the creation of new brain cells; and actually activates systems that strengthen brain circuits.

Of course, before you jump into any kind of physical exercise program, check with your doctor.

The folks at SharpBrains.com recommend at least 15 minutes of daily exercise—the best are cardiovascular exercises, those that get your heart beating faster. These exercises can include such activities as biking, walking, running, swimming, hiking, tennis, basketball, touch football, ultimate Frisbee, and similar sports/activities.

Here's what our students have to say:

"The brain is like any other muscle. When you're in top physical shape, your brain just works better. I find I do better in school when I'm also playing tennis." —Peter D.

"I started working out as an attempt to prevent the 'freshmen 15,' going to the gym a few times a week. When reading magazines got old, I started taking my class notes to the gym. Running the bicycles, walking the treadmill, or jogging the elliptical, I casually skimmed my notes without any effort of trying to study. When I went to class, I was amazed at all the concepts I had remembered from *not studying* at the gym. Just by simply casually reading these items while working out, your brain is engaged more than usual and more susceptible to retain information and recall it later in class. It's almost impossible to read a textbook while working out, so I suggest something basic, like class notes. You read a few points and ponder them, then move on. I follow that workout with some cardio to relieve stress, followed by a small protein snack while reading the textbook—your senses are still alert—and I can retain anything I read from a new chapter in the textbook." —Adrianne W.

In terms of nutrition—something many college students ignore— SharpBrains.com recommends planning meals around vegetables, then adding fruit, protein, dairy, and/or grains. The website stresses:

"If you can only do one thing, eat more vegetables, particularly leafy green ones." Other experts recommend passing on the soda and instead drinking water, which they say helps your brain stay focused. Finally, other experts recommend increasing your intake of essential fatty acids known as omega-3, which can be found in fish oils, nuts, and seeds, to improve your brain-functioning abilities.

WebMD.com offers a brain food quiz to test your knowledge of which foods can help boost memory. Find it here: www.webmd.com/content/tools/1/brain_food_quiz.htm.

"I recommend that students take healthy study breaks and try to eat nutritional foods to stay healthy." —Morgan S.

"I can also only study when I'm fully comfortable—so I always have to remember to eat before studying." —Jessica W.

What You've Learned

Ready for a quick check to see what you've learned from this chapter? I now understand ...

- ◆ Whenever it's possible, it's much better to study in small chunks rather than one long period.

- ◆ It's a good idea to review previous tests and assignments so I have a better idea of what to expect.

- ◆ I need to find a study system that works best for my academic goals.

- ◆ A great way to improve my performance and better understand assignments is to meet with my professors.

- ◆ There appears to be a connection between physical fitness and brain fitness, and I should try to keep physically active to stay mentally active.

You're now ready to move into Part 2 of the book—and the first part of the TEST Method. Here you'll learn key strategies for taking responsibility for your learning.

The Least You Need to Know

- ◆ Multiple study systems exist, and the most important thing is to find what works for you.

- ◆ The best source for classroom expectations and tips on improving your performance is your professor.

- ◆ Paying attention to your physical fitness and nutrition will help your brain perform at a higher capacity.

Part 2

Taking Responsibility for Learning

Do you struggle with deadlines and getting everything done on time? Have you found that some classes are much easier for you to understand than others? Do you feel overwhelmed by all the reading you've been assigned?

The chapters in this part are designed to help you better handle time management and avoid procrastination, discover and use your learning style, and learn to complete your reading assignments strategically.

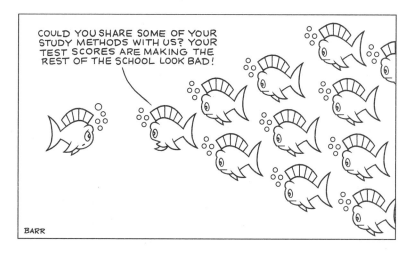

Chapter 4

Time Management and Organizational Systems

In This Chapter

- ◆ Learn to conquer procrastination
- ◆ Discover the basics of managing your time
- ◆ Choose a time-management system that works for you
- ◆ See how to squeeze more productivity from your time

Of all the new challenges you will face when you start college, few are as challenging as managing your time and staying organized. The freedom you find in college may be very different from what you are used to, and you might find this new way of life quite difficult to adapt to.

At the same time, you suddenly have a new array of demands on your time—a much greater study expectation than in high school, a new social life, extracurricular activities, sports, and perhaps a job. Balancing all these activities can make your head spin.

This chapter offers techniques for organizing your time and your life, and avoiding the paralysis—known as procrastination—that sets in when you become overwhelmed.

Avoiding Procrastination and Taking Responsibility

If you tend to procrastinate, you are far from alone among college students. Research indicates that 40 percent of college students put off important academic tasks. Surprisingly, procrastination is not directly related to time management; it's linked to psychological blocks we put in place when faced with unpleasant, stressful, complex, or unfamiliar activities. Procrastinators *know* how they should be using their time; they simply place barriers in the way of doing so.

Study Stories

"I am a very busy person. I think that outside activities are just as important to succeed in college as studying and staying strong academically, so my advice is: stay organized, and make sure you have time to have fun and to study!"

—Jessica W.

Some procrastination is the result of having unrealistic expectations about how long a project will take to complete, which is a particular problem for new college students who are not accustomed to the magnitude of college projects. Experience and the time-tracking activity suggested later in this chapter should help you develop more realistic estimates of the time needed for assignments.

As a procrastinator, you may also fool yourself into believing that you do your best work under pressure, a belief that tends to be reinforced if your last-minute work results in good grades. But the moment will come when your rushed effort suddenly isn't good enough, and you land in deep trouble.

Another common college-student procrastination rationalization is that you aren't in the right mood or frame of mind to do your work. Or you are a perfectionist who cannot finish a project unless you feel it is flawless. Many other root causes, both simple and complex, underlie procrastination. If you tend to procrastinate, you may find it helpful to ask yourself, "Why am I putting off working on this project?"

Experts recommend a number of techniques for overcoming procrastination:

Tiny chunks of time: If you can't bring yourself to plunge into the whole assignment, commit to doing what you can accomplish in a very short period—5, 10, 15 minutes. Mary McKinney of Successful Academic Coaching refers to the "Tolerable 10," 10 relatively painless minutes devoted to your project. Of course, the bonus here is that may find yourself so caught up in the assignment once you put in those few minutes that you will continue working on it.

Motivation by doing it: If you're one of those who feels unmotivated or is in the wrong mood, simply beginning the project may give you the motivation you need to keep going. You'll feel better about yourself and the assignment.

Committed self-talk: Tell yourself before you go to bed at night that you will spend X amount of time tomorrow on your project. Remind yourself of that goal when you get up in the morning.

> **Study Stories**
>
> "If you're going to procrastinate, don't just watch TV; do something, like grocery shopping, that you would need to do anyway."
>
> —Erin L.

Regular meetings with your professor: This technique works especially well with semester-long projects. Ask if you can meet with your professor regularly—every couple of weeks or so—to show him or her your progress on your project and ensure that you're on the right track. Because you will be accountable to your teacher, you will have to reach your planned benchmarks.

If you have procrastinated and find yourself in a bind, step up and take responsibility for your deficiency. Talk to your professor. Say that you messed up and ask for help developing a plan to get the project done. It's extremely helpful in this situation to have at least *some* of the project completed. Show your professor what you've done, and explain that you feel you could improve it enormously if you had just one more day to work on it. You may have to weigh the degree to which you feel you can improve the paper against any possible penalty for a late paper. Let's say that you estimate the paper you've written is a D paper that you feel capable of turning into a B paper—but the instructor's policy is that every day of lateness means a drop in letter grade. If your predictions about the paper are on target, you'll end up with a C, which is better than a D—so the extension is worthwhile. Be prepared, however, for inflexibility from your professor. Some instructors may give you a "get out of jail free" card for the first offense, but many other profs feel strongly that a deadline is a deadline, and that it's not fair to your classmates for you to get a break. If your instructor won't agree to an extension, ask if you can later rework the paper after it has been graded, to improve your grade. And be sure to promise that your irresponsibility won't happen again.

Quick and dirty assignment completion: This technique is for when other procrastination-avoidance methods have failed, but the sands in the hourglass of your assignment deadline haven't quite run out. If you haven't organized up to this point, sketch out a quick outline or its equivalent of the assignment now. At the very least, have a good handle on the purpose of the assignment—your main point or thesis. A technique that can work for you and get you started is writing by speaking; just write as you speak, type as you write, and save the assignment often as you type. As a colleague points out, "Computers seem to know when you're under pressure." Let your anxiety work for you instead of against you. Don't let time terrorize you; let it empower you. Remember that producing an assignment in a time-pressured environment is a lot like taking an essay exam. As long as you know your material (or at least have your material close at hand) while remaining cool and confident, you can pull it off.

Once you've diagnosed your procrastination and taken steps to overcome it, you'll find many of the time-management tips and systems in this chapter helpful.

Tackling Time Management

Many students become overwhelmed with managing their time when they start college, ironically not because they have so little time available, but because they have so much time—and so much more freedom.

Unlike high school, in which you were sequestered in classrooms for perhaps seven hours a day, in college you may have large blocks of time or even entire days without classes. And you have no parents around to remind you when to do things and to play a role in planning your time.

Before we get into specific time-management systems that may work for you, here are some general tips:

Track your time: To get a good feel for where your time is going, spend a week writing down *everything* you do, hour by hour. You will begin to develop a feel for ways you are using time effectively, as well as how you are wasting time on unproductive activities. You may be surprised by the number of time-wasters you can cut from your schedule.

Set realistic goals: Once you start to get a feel for how long it takes you to complete assignments and study effectively for tests, you can build those times into your planning. Keep tracking your time as you progress through school so you'll know if, for example, allotting a month for a big project or two weeks to study for finals is sufficient. And remember that if you've followed advice elsewhere in this book to study as you go along, you should be able to set realistic goals to prepare for tests.

Multiply time estimates by up to threefold: Those realistic goals you just set? Some experts—and students—recommend multiplying the time needed to meet any academic goal by 1.5, 2, or even 3, depending on the complexity of the test or assignment. Allotting much more time than needed will allow for unexpected interruptions, distractions, and miscalculations of how long the work will actually take.

Avoid procrastination with an easy-to-remember system: Just recall the first letters of the days of the week using the technique proposed by Dave Ellis in *Becoming a Master Student:*

> **Monday** = **M**ake It **M**eaningful: List the benefits and payoff of accomplishing the task (such as a good grade).

> **Tuesday** = **T**ake It Apart: Break the task into pieces you can accomplish in a short period.

> **Wednesday** = **W**rite It Down: Commit your intention to accomplish the task to writing.

Thursday = Tell Everyone: Make yourself accountable to others by telling them your intention. You'll have to face them if you don't do it. A similar tactic is to join a study group so its members can motivate you to work (see Chapter 8).

Friday = Find a Reward: Reward yourself by accomplishing all or part of the task.

Saturday = Settle It Now. This is the "just do it" step.

Sunday = Say No. In this step, having tried all the others, you face the fact that you are not going to get the task done. While this one should not be an option in your academic life, be prepared to talk to your professor, take responsibility, and accept the consequences if it happens.

Study Suggestions

The University of Minnesota offers an awesome tool—an Assignment Calculator at www.lib.umn.edu/help/calculator—that enables you to type in the day you're starting an assignment, enter the due date, and indicate the type of class. The result is a timetable by which you can tackle each project component. You can even sign up for e-mail reminders of benchmark dates. The timetable contains links with more information about how to tackle various parts of assignments.

Break tasks into smaller components: This advice, touched on in other parts of this book, is about determining all the smaller component tasks of larger projects and study demands. Chapter 12 suggests a timetable for breaking down a semester-long research paper into component parts, but here we look at a sample timetable for a shorter-term writing assignment, a five-page English paper on a specific piece of literature due in two weeks. Here's how your timetable might look:

Jan. 15	Receive assignment
Jan. 15–17	Develop and finalize topic/thesis
Jan. 17–20	Conduct reading, research

Jan. 20–23	Plan organization of paper; do outline, if necessary
Jan. 23–25	Write rough draft
Jan. 25–30	Edit, revise, and polish final draft; do bibliography, if necessary

Get the hardest tasks—or the easiest—out of the way first: For assignments that don't have to be completed in sequence, or for an array of tasks relating to several assignments, many experts recommend doing the hardest ones first, to get them over with. You'll have a downhill coast from there. Others prefer to tackle the easy chores first because they can be handled quickly and without too much angst. Because you accomplished part of the project right away, you may be motivated to keep going, even though the toughest tasks are still ahead of you. It's actually a form of procrastination to put off the hardest components, but it's productive procrastination.

 Study Stories

"Believe it or not, my secret is to stay busy. I feel like the more down time I have, the more I procrastinate. I worked my entire college career, and it forced me to manage my time effectively."

—Dana S.

Stay as busy as possible: This advice may sound counterintuitive, but keeping a very active schedule will make you a better time manager. When our daughter was in high school, her grades were always better in the fall, when she was competing on the swim team, than in the spring, when she didn't know what to do with her extra time. Similarly, the first-year baseball

 Study Stories

"I find that if I have nothing to do on a certain day, I am less likely to get things done. If I have a set schedule and a set place to be, I make sure I have things done in order to get the next project done or go to the next event I have for the day."

—Emily B.

players we had in our fall classes were lost when fall practices were over and they had vast chunks of time they didn't know how to manage. Not only will involvement in campus activities or a job make you a better time manager, but this will help you build your resumé with experience and well-roundedness that will impress employers.

Time-Management and Project-Management Systems

While the preceding time-management strategies will help you wrestle the time-management monster, you probably won't have complete control of your time unless you find a system of managing time and projects that works for you. Following are several systems that students swear by. Experiment to find the system or combination of systems that works best for you:

Determine priorities: Several techniques are available for determining your priorities.

Consider creating a matrix to determine priorities, and list projects in the cells of the matrix. A simple one looks like this:

High importance		High importance
Low difficulty	|	High difficulty
	|	
	|	
	|	
------------------------------		----------------------------
Low difficulty	|	High difficulty
Low importance	|	Low importance
	|	
	|	

Obviously, you'd want to do the highly important but not very difficult activities first. The highly difficult but highly important tasks also need to be done but may need more planning. You might consider eliminating any of the low-importance activities, especially those that are highly difficult.

Another commonly used method is to assign letters to each task: A for the most urgent, B for important items, and C for those not as pressing as the A and B items. C items will likely be those outside your schoolwork, such as extracurricular and social obligations. Then assign numbers for the tasks in each category. The most urgent item in the A category would be A1, and so on.

To a great extent, the urgency of each item will be determined by deadlines, due dates, and test dates listed on your syllabi. Be flexible; you'll sometimes need to shift priorities. If you find that you are never getting to the C items, you may need to drop them or reconsider your commitment to the organization they are associated with. Another strategy is to try to block out a day periodically to take care of all the C tasks at once.

Study Stressors

In prioritizing your activities—or in developing any time-management system—don't spend so much time working on the system itself that you take away time from more urgent demands. Find a system that you can maintain efficiently and easily. Assume that you'll learn from trial and error, and don't sweat coming up with a perfect system.

A third way to organize priorities is to list what must be done today, followed by what must be done this week, this month, and by the end of the semester.

Make a to-do list on steroids: Choose a period of time that's workable for you—today, this week, this month, this semester—and list everything

Study Stories

"Don't just make a list of things that you need to do each day in your agenda; actually do them and then cross them off your list so that you can move on to something else."

—Cayla C.

you need to do. Then prioritize the items on your list according to the preceding criteria. One great advantage of a to-do list is the satisfaction that comes from crossing items off your list.

You can make a to-do list even more powerful by combining it with other methods in this chapter:

◆ Estimate the time it will take you to accomplish each item, and multiply by up to threefold.

◆ Pull individual entries from your list and make separate to-do lists for *each* item—listing component parts of each.

◆ Assign specific time blocks to each activity.

◆ Instead of making a to-do list of activities, develop a list of academic objectives (such as earning an A on an exam) and then develop a list of tasks you'll need to accomplish to meet the objective and how long each task will take (multiplying by up to threefold).

Study Stories

"My biggest secret is my planner! I would die without it! I write everything in it and cross it off when it's done. It gives me a sense of accomplishment and makes me get things done and remember to do them."

—Emily B.

Use a daily, weekly, monthly, or semesterly planner: More students rely on a planner than on any other kind of time-management tool. Planners come in many styles and are usually in the form of small books that you carry with you everywhere.

Planners come with pages broken down by day, week, or month. You'll need to choose which format works best for you, and you may also need a combination—say, pages broken down by day to see what you need to do in a given day, but also including a monthly view so you can see looming deadlines.

Also decide how much you will write down in your planner. To what extent do you need to schedule your time? Do you need just a bare-bones outline of what you need to do, or do you need a finely detailed schedule?

Study Stories

"As crazy as it may sound, make hour-by-hour schedules for the day. When I get a minute free or right before a class starts, I will open my planner and write down everything I have to do the next day and the times. Then I write down the hours 10 A.M. to 1 A.M. and fill them in. This lets me know what spots I have free so that I can fill them with homework, errands, etc."

—Maria F.

At the very least, you'll want to scrutinize all your syllabi as soon as your professors give them to you and enter all assignment due dates and tests in your planner. You'll probably want to enter your work schedule and meeting times for extracurricular activities and practice/game times for sports, as well as other appointments. You may want to update your planner at least weekly, perhaps at the same time each week.

To succeed with a planner, you have to open it, look at it, and make frequent entries in it. That's why some students prefer a less portable but more visible system, such as a large calendar at their desks. You can't take it with you, but it's right there in your face every time you're working at your desk. This type of planner is especially good for viewing one or more months at a time or a full semester. If you prefer a nonportable calendar/planner, take a small notebook to class with you so you can write down due dates and assignments to transfer to the calendar in your room.

Study Stories

"One thing that works really well for me is to write everything down. I mean everything! I write down if I am going to e-mail people, write letters, or study."

—Laura B.

Add color coding: Numerous students have discovered that color-coding activities in their planners helps them organize their time-planning better and see at a glance which category each activity falls into. You could also use colors to indicate priority levels for each activity.

Use a personal digital assistant (PDA) device: More students are using electronic gadgets, such as Palm, BlackBerry, Pocket PC, Treo, and Smart Phone, in the same way they once used paper planners. Features available on these devices vary widely, but basics usually include the capability to keep to-do lists, maintain a calendar, and record addresses and phone numbers. These devices are even more portable than paper planners since they're smaller and they hold more information. Depending on the device, additional accessories and the availability of thousands of software applications can expand the PDA's capabilities in many ways that can help you academically. Some of these capabilities include creating word-processing documents, spreadsheets, databases, and presentations; taking notes; providing reminders through alarms; receiving and/or sending e-mail; displaying e-books that you can read; creating files and folders; playing music; enabling game-playing; taking and/or storing photos; interfacing with computers and other devices; communicating with other PDAs through "beaming"; and accessing the Internet. To review a comparison table and determine whether a PDA suits your work style, see www.trapperwoods.com/timemanagement/loworhightech.cfm.

Study Suggestions

You can find all kinds of calendars that may help you plan your time at CalendarsThatWork.com. Twenty-two types of calendars are available for download (in Microsoft Word) at no cost. A larger variety is available for an annual fee of less than $20.

Study Stories

"I use different color highlighters to show what each event on my calendar is for. For example, pink is personal, yellow is school, orange is work, blue is for appointments, and green is for my sorority .... I can see in bright yellow that I have that project for finance due on Tuesday, and I need to start working on it on Wednesday so I can just get it done. My friends have always been amazed at how early I get things accomplished, but that is really all I do."

—Sarah P.

Making the Most of Your Time

After minimizing procrastination and developing a system for managing your time, you can squeeze out even more time-management efficiency through these techniques:

Explore the amount of available time and allot a portion to schoolwork: Ever wish there were more hours in the day? How many hours are available, anyway? Of the 168 hours in a week, 84 are used for such necessary activities as sleeping, eating, bathing, primping, and commuting, says Brian Poser of New York University. That leaves 84 hours.

Professors recommend two to three hours of out-of-class study time for each hour of class time—up to 45 hours a week of study time for 15 hours of classes. Similarly, some suggest that students equate their college education to a full-time job—40 hours a week minus actual class time, resulting in 25 hours of study time for a 15-credit-hour load.

You must then decide how to divide up that available study time—and then determine how to fit in extracurricular activities, sports, socializing, and "me time." Will you spread out your study time over five days, six days, seven days, or some other configuration?

Don't forget about school holidays and breaks. While these are largely for relaxing and recharging your batteries, you may want to schedule at least some schoolwork during times of no classes.

 **Study Stories**

"I try to get my schedule at work to be the same each week so that I always know when I have to work and am able to plan my homework and other responsibilities into the time I have."

—Cayla C.

Study Stories

"I distribute all my assignments throughout the week based on how much time I'll have left after class, activities, and other obligations. Usually, I try to leave room for surprise assignments so that I have some flexibility in case something pops up that I didn't anticipate."

—Stephanie G.

Examining the available time is a good way to determine how much time you can devote to a job. Deduct the time you'd need for a job from your free time rather than from your study time. If you're unwilling to give up that much free time and you don't absolutely have to hold a job, you may decide against getting one.

Identify your most productive times: Once you've calculated exactly how much time you have available for schoolwork, determine the days of the week and times of the day when you are at your best and most productive. You may discover that your best day is simply the one with the most available time, but it may be more a matter of mood or mental attitude. For example, many students do a lot of work on Sunday, while others aren't in the right frame of mind on Sunday because they dread Monday. And do you do your best work in the morning, in the evening, or in the middle of the day? Many find the early part of the day to be the most productive—with the added psychological bonus of clearing your decks for the rest of the day. You must determine what time works best for you and capitalize on the days and times when you can get the most done.

Study Stories

"Since I usually work about 25 to 35 hours a week (and during my sophomore year, I worked 45 hours a week) and take 15 credit hours, I try to do my homework at night and in the mornings. Since my weekends are spent working, I tell myself that I will do all my assignments for next week during the current week. This can get difficult because it is hard to sit down and work on homework after sitting through three classes back to back."

—Morgan S.

Determine your concentration span: How long can you realistically study before your attention fades? Twenty minutes? Fifty minutes? Track your concentration span. You may need to schedule studying in relatively small chunks of time to ensure that you continue to absorb the material. Another option is big study blocks with short breaks and rewards built in to help you recharge.

Capitalize on waiting times, break times, and travel/commuting times: You will encounter numerous situations in college life when you are waiting around—waiting in line, waiting for a bus, waiting for your next class to start. Use those times to your best advantage. Always have at least one textbook and some class notes with you to read anytime you find yourself in a waiting situation. Do you take a bus or train to classes? Read or study then. If you drive, you can record notes to listen to on a tape player or MP3 player (may require a microphone accessory). See if any of your required texts (especially novels that you might be assigned in English and literature classes) are available as audiobooks that you can listen to while waiting. Apply these same techniques to longer trips, such as flights or drives home on breaks from school. Consider even making productive use of the time you spend in the bathroom; read in the tub or on the commode.

Conduct before-class, after-class, and weekly reviews of course material: As mentioned in Chapter 8, conducting regular reviews of your notes and readings keeps you from having to cram, but doing so also helps you manage your time by ensuring that free time surrounding your classes is productively spent. Review your notes before each class when pockets of time allow, and review notes for all of a day's classes at the end of the day.

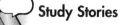

Study Stories

"If I know that on a particular day I don't have any time at all, then I will wake up earlier and get in some studying time then. I also know myself enough to not schedule studying for late at night since I won't be able to stay awake."

—Jessica H.

Study Stories

"I always reward myself. If I don't let myself watch my favorite television show or something, then I get easily distracted while studying. I can't study for great lengths at a time, so I make sure to take little breaks."

—Renee P.

Earmark a timeslot over the weekend to review all your notes from the previous week.

Avoid distractions, especially of the electronic variety: If you track the time you spend checking e-mail, searching the Internet (including checking up on MySpace and Facebook), instant-messaging, and texting your friends, you might be horrified by how much time you spend on these electronic distractions. Discipline yourself to pursue these activities for limited periods just a few times a day. These are excellent activities to use as rewards for reaching your study goals. To minimize temptation, unplug your computer's network cable or disable its mechanism for connecting to wireless networks. During intensive study periods, turn off your cell phone.

> **Study Stories**
>
> "My time-management secret is not to take naps during the day or waste time. I get most of my work done in between classes and during the day so my nights can sometimes be free."
>
> —Nicole Z.

What You've Learned

Ready for a quick check to see what you've learned from this chapter? I now understand ...

- That procrastination is normal but not hard to overcome.

- Basic principles of time management.

- How to choose a time-management system that best suits my style.

- Ways I can be even more productive.

The Least You Need to Know

- You can conquer procrastination, which is rampant among college students and not even directly related to time management.

- When students understand how they spend their time and how much time they need to get schoolwork done, they've taken an important step toward time management.

◆ No one perfect time-management system exists for students; each student must choose the one that works best, and trial-and-error may be needed.

◆ Students can enhance their time-management systems by learning even more ways to make their time productive.

5

Finding Your Learning Style

In This Chapter

- Determine your preferred learning style
- Discover how to make the most of your learning style
- Learn how to avoid learning-style pitfalls
- Solve problems with successful intelligence

Everyone learns a bit differently. We all have preferences in the way we take in information. Researchers have developed several schemes to categorize the various ways of learning, and learning-style theory does not seem to favor any one scheme. Learning styles can encompass how you manage information so you'll remember it, how you prefer to study, and how you go about solving problems.

Some people don't predominately fit into any one learning style, but they learn in multiple ways. No one style of learning is better or worse than any other; however, some learning styles mesh better with how teaching is typically conducted in the college classroom.

This chapter focuses on the most common set of learning-style categories: visual, auditory, and kinesthetic/tactile, based on the Barsch Learning-Style Inventory. We also include global and sequential/analytic learning styles from the Index of Learning Styles (ILS) scheme.

For each of these learning styles, the chapter offers overall characteristics, in-class strategies, and study strategies. We also suggest the types of courses you might want to select for their suitability to your learning style. Now, obviously, you will not always have the luxury of choosing classes that match your learning style—nor is it easy to find out whether various classes offer the characteristics that fit your style. But you will clearly stack the deck in your favor if you can identify at least a few classes during your college career that work particularly well with the way you learn. To find out about characteristics, ask around among your friends and talk to professors. If you take a class that meshes well with your learning preference, consider taking more classes with that professor.

Finally, this chapter asks you to assess the thinking skills you use to solve problems and offers tips to improve analytical, creative, and practical thinking skills.

Determining Your Learning Style

You may find it extremely useful to identify your learning style so you can make the most of it to succeed in school. Once you grasp your learning style, you'll probably develop a much greater understanding of any problems you've had with academic success. Be aware that your preference may be for a mix of styles. One style may dominate, with another closely behind—or perhaps no one style stands out because you like several ways of learning.

You can find a number of free online assessments and inventories to help you determine your preferred learning style or styles. To determine where you fit on the Barsch visual, auditory, and kinesthetic/tactile scale, try these assessments:

- www.metamath.com/multiple/multiple_choice_questions.html
- www.ldpride.net/learning_style.html

◆ www.howtolearn.com/styles.html

◆ www.2learn.org/learningstyles.html

For a very quick way to determine your style, see the chart at www. chaminade.org/inspire/learnstl.htm.

The ILS scheme measures categories that include active versus reflective learning, sensing versus intuitive learning, visual versus verbal learning, and sequential (also called analytical) versus global learning. You can assess yourself based on these categories at www.engr.ncsu. edu/learningstyles/ilsweb.html and learn more about them at www4. ncsu.edu/unity/lockers/users/f/felder/public/ILSdir/styles.htm and www.vmentor.com/docs/learning_styles_module.pdf.

The Multiple Intelligences Inventory consists of linguistic, mathematics, visual/spatial, body/kinesthetic, naturalistic, music, interpersonal, and intrapersonal assessments. You can assess yourself based on these categories at www.ldrc.ca/projects/miinventory/miinventory.php and learn more about them at www.ldrc.ca/projects/miinventory/miinventory.php?eightstyles=1.

Still another set is found in the Memletics Learning Styles Inventory, encompassing visual, aural, verbal, physical, logical, social, and solitary learning styles. You can assess yourself based on these categories at www.learning-styles-online.com/inventory/ and learn more about them at www.learning-styles-online.com/overview.

Study Suggestions

The concept of "learning style" also deals with your environmental preferences for learning. Knowing these preferences will help you work more effectively. Do you like it quiet when you study, or must you have a lot of background noise? Do you prefer bright lights or soft, dim ones? Does a formal setting such as a desk and chair work for you, or are you just as effective studying in your bed? Do you like to move around? Do you need a great deal of structure in the instructions you receive about assignments, or does a lot of structure make you feel suffocated? Do you prefer to study alone, or do you need to study with others?

Visual Learners

Visual learners prefer to take in information through sight and like to learn through reading, diagrams, charts, graphs, maps, and pictures. They can easily mentally "see" facts and concepts, and are said to be able to recall at least 75 percent of material read or observed.

Considering that the greatest number of people—about 60 percent—are visual learners, most classrooms are surprisingly devoid of visual-learning stimuli. Many classes primarily feature the "talking head" of the professor lecturing or the full class engaged in discussion, but not much that is compelling to a visual learner.

Class selection: Visual learners should consider classes with strong multimedia (especially visual) elements, such as PowerPoint presentations and films. Look into online classes or classes that are taught in computer labs. Consider graphic design classes. Art history classes should mesh well with your visual style. You will likely succeed in classes with writing assignments. Math classes based on geometry suit your style more than those based on algebra. If more than one section of a class is offered, go to the campus bookstore to view the texts assigned for each section. Choose the section with the most visually interesting textbooks. Note that college classes are offered in various lengths of time, such as 50 minutes, 75 minutes, 90 minutes, and 2 or 3 hours. Visual learners may become frustrated with having to listen to professors talk for long periods and may be better off taking classes that last for shorter periods, when possible. Seek out professors who like to communicate via e-mail, distribute handouts (especially with illustrations), provide outlines of their lectures, give written feedback, and write copiously on the board.

In-class strategies:

◆ Sit in front of the class so you can watch the professor and get a good view of any visuals presented. Observe body language, hand gestures, and facial expressions.

◆ Take detailed notes (see Chapter 7). Consider taking notes on graph paper so you can easily add charts and diagrams.

◆ Include visual representa-
tions in your notes. Include,
of course, any visuals that
the professor draws on the
board, but also invent your
own illustrations of con-
cepts and draw them as part
of your notes.

 Study Stressors

Be careful about day-
dreaming in class, since your
natural tendency is to have
visions dancing in your head.

Study strategies:

◆ Study from the notes you've taken, but also consider typing them.
Use spreadsheet and presentation software programs to help you
organize information visually.

◆ Use flash cards (see Chapters 6 and 8).

◆ Use mind maps (see Chapter 8).

◆ Develop outlines, charts, tables, and other ways to visually represent concepts to be studied (see Chapters 6 and 8).

◆ Close your eyes and create mental pictures to remember aspects of
reading assignments and lectures (see Chapter 6).

◆ Use color-coding in your time-management system (see Chapter 4)
and in highlighting reading assignments (see Chapter 6).

◆ Annotate as you read (see Chapter 6), especially using symbols
and pictures to help you remember what you read.

◆ Write or make diagrams for all the steps for activities such as
math problems.

◆ Look for opportunities to supplement the visual aspects of your
learning. For example, many classics of literature have been made
into films. Look in your campus library for films of the books you
read in English and literature classes. Also ask your professors if
any films are available about the concepts you're studying in other
classes. Look on the Internet at sites such as YouTube for video
clips that might enhance your learning.

- Study in an environment with interesting things to look at but without noise interruptions. While a visually stimulating environment would be distracting to some, visual learners may lose focus without the stimulus.

- Use visualization to confront study anxieties and fears. A method known as the swish technique works well for visual learners. See http://hypnosense.com/swish_technique.htm.

Auditory Learners

Auditory learners prefer to absorb information through their sense of hearing. They tend to be fond of speaking out loud, talking to themselves, and listening to themselves talk. They have difficulty handling distracting noises. They like to talk through issues and problems, and prefer to hear directions verbally. They may become bored when classroom activities are solitary and silent, such as during in-class writing assignments. They are said to be able to recall at least 75 percent of material they hear. About 30 percent of learners have the auditory learning-style preference.

Class selection: Auditory learners should look for classes with hefty discussion elements. Try to enroll in small classes, to increase your opportunities to be called on and join in the class discussion. Seek out professors who are open to being asked a lot of questions and who will give you verbal feedback. Do you know of a professor who sprinkles lectures with stories and anecdotes? Perfect for you! You will likely excel in classes that require public speaking, presentations, and perhaps even debate. Foreign languages and music will also probably be relatively easy for you.

In-class strategies:

- Sit in a part of the classroom where you can hear well.

- Privately ask the professor to intervene if classmates constantly talk in class and distract you, or if other noise creates distractions.

- Be sure to copy notes from the board as accurately as possible, since your tendency is not to.

◆ Ask questions to clarify information.

◆ In classes in which lecture material aligns very closely with reading assignments, you may want to listen to the lecture first and then reinforce your learning by reading the corresponding chapter. Similarly, lecture outlines provided by your professor will enable you to devote full attention to your best skill, listening, while taking minimal notes.

 **Study Stressors**

Be careful not to annoy your professor by talking to classmates when the professor is talking. That's your natural tendency, since you like to chat and hear yourself talk.

Study strategies:

◆ Ask others to explain things you don't understand.

◆ Join study groups so you can discuss class material and hear others discuss it (see Chapter 8).

◆ Teach material to others.

◆ Recite or speak your notes aloud (see Chapter 6).

◆ Use mnemonics (see Chapter 8).

◆ Create story and anecdote versions of study material, and read them to yourself.

◆ Record your notes and play them back.

◆ Ask your professor to permit you to record lectures.

◆ Make up silly sayings or musical jingles to help you remember material.

◆ Talk your way through activities such as math problems.

◆ Look for audio recordings and podcasts to enhance your learning. Check out, for example, iTunesU,

Study Stressors

It's typical for an auditory learner to want a classmate to verbally confirm details of an assignment, but a better source for getting these aspects explained to you is your professor.

which offers podcast presentations, performances, lectures, demonstrations, debates, tours, and archival footage from more than 250 universities.

Kinesthetic/Tactile Learners

Kinesthetic/tactile learners prefer to take in information through movement, manipulation, and touch. They tend to be able to operate equipment without reading instructions. They can easily learn dance steps and athletic maneuvers. About 5 percent of learners are kinesthetic/tactile.

Class selection: Kinesthetic/tactile learners should try to identify classes that involve role-play, simulations, and major projects outside class. Look for classes with hands-on activities and demonstrations (in which you get to do some of the demos). You will likely succeed in science classes that have a lab component, as well as dance, theater, and physical education classes. You'll probably enjoy studio-art classes. You will also do well in any type of experiential learning, including internships. Try a class in American Sign Language.

In-class strategies:

◆ Since your natural inclination is to move around or even fidget in class, find ways to move that are not disruptive to the class, such as by doodling as you take notes or chewing gum.

Study Stressors

Avoid movements, such as pencil-tapping, foot-tapping, or jingling coins and keys in your pocket. That may be your natural inclination, but it may distract classmates and your teacher.

◆ Try the relaxation techniques described in Chapter 14 before classes to help control your tendency to fidget.

◆ Simply taking notes is a good way to keep moving in class.

◆ If a teacher asks for a volunteer to demonstrate something in front of the class, you're the ideal candidate.

Study strategies:

◆ Move around while studying. Walk, run, or work out with recorded notes playing on an MP3 player.

◆ When you're not moving, study in a very relaxed position, such as lying down. You won't be comfortable sitting at a desk.

◆ Active reading strategies (see Chapter 6), such as highlighting and making flash cards, will work well for you, with the actual physical activity involved being one of the most helpful aspects. The same goes for rewriting and typing your notes.

◆ Write study material on large surfaces, such as easel pads and whiteboards, in large letters. Again, the physical act of writing the material appeals to your learning style.

◆ Identify with historical and literary characters in your reading assignments. Immerse yourself in those characters and become involved in the readings by *being* the characters.

◆ Put yourself in the role of your instructor and imagine how you'd teach the material, what questions you'd ask, and what you'd include on exams.

◆ Manipulate magnetic poetry words (www.magneticpoetry.com) to get ideas for writing assignments.

◆ Draw or create three-dimensional models to illustrate concepts to be studied.

◆ Use sticky notes to take notes while reading (see Chapter 6).

◆ Study in short segments, taking frequent breaks.

◆ Keep your hands busy by playing with, for example, a squishy ball while studying. Another way to stay active while sitting still is to chew gum (sugarless is a good idea).

◆ Practice new skills you've learned.

◆ Seek opportunities to experience real-life examples of topics you're studying about, such as in museums and at historical sites.

Global vs. Analytical/Sequential Learners

The learning styles of global and analytical/sequential learners overlap with visual, auditory, and kinesthetic/tactile learners. In other words, you can be a visual learner and also a global learner, for example.

You can learn more about global versus analytical/sequential learners at these sites:

◆ www4.ncsu.edu/unity/lockers/users/f/felder/public/ILSdir/styles.htm

◆ www.helium.com/tm/352978/sequential-learning-learning-information

◆ www.ministrytba.com/learning_style.htm

Global Learners

Global learners are intuitive decision makers for whom interpersonal connections are important. They like to take their time when learning and think things through. They may have emotional responses to learning. They like to learn through stories and anecdotes, and can often imagine what happens next. They tend to see the big picture and overlook details. They can solve complex problems and put things together in innovative ways, but they have trouble explaining how they did it. They often don't see connections right away, but then suddenly everything clicks.

Class selection: Global learners will enjoy classes that are very conceptual and involve lots of imagery, such as literature, philosophy, psychology, and religion. Try to take classes that interest you immensely. Enroll in classes that entail group projects. Seek professors who will give you significant feedback and who have a good sense of humor. Since you need help in connecting new concepts to past learning, it may help you to take several classes with the same professor. Look for colorful textbooks.

In-class strategies:

- ◆ Pay particular attention to the beginnings of lectures, which set the tone and help you see the big picture of what will be said.

- ◆ If the professor is explaining a concept you don't understand, ask for an example.

- ◆ Talk to your professor if you are having difficulty seeing how course components connect.

- ◆ Ask your professor for samples of assignments.

 Study Stressors _____

Be careful in classes that require significant participation. You often miss the opportunity to participate because you are thinking about what you want to say. Sometimes you'll need to take a risk and raise your hand before you've thought through your comment or answer.

Study strategies:

- ◆ Surveying reading material before you read it will help you tremendously (see Chapter 6).

- ◆ Blocks of study time that are relatively long and devoted to one subject at a time mesh well with the global learner's style. For example, you may want to devote each night of study to a given subject. However, global learners also need to take frequent breaks.

- ◆ You will probably be able to multitask while studying and can tolerate noise.

- ◆ You will be comfortable studying in dim light.

- ◆ Study groups suit your style (see Chapter 8).

- ◆ Though you will be tempted to skip steps in projects that require them, you may not always be able to do so. Your inclination is to avoid asking for explanations, but you may prevent mistakes if you do ask.

Study Stressors _____

Be careful in tests, such as in math, in which you are required to show your steps. Your natural inclination is to dislike dealing with the steps, but your grade may depend on doing so.

◆ Be careful with time management (see Chapter 4). With your tendency to think things through slowly and deliberately, you may find time slipping away from you.

Analytical/Sequential Learners

These learners prefer linear steps that logically follow each other. Analytical/sequential learners prefer working on projects in small chunks. They can discern details but often have trouble seeing the big picture.

Class selection: Analytical/sequential learners will thrive in classes that are always taught in a sequential manner, such as math, science, history, and languages. If you hear of a professor who jumps around and does not follow a logical order in presenting material, you may want to avoid him or her.

In-class strategies:

◆ Sit in the front of the class so you won't be distracted by student activity in front of you.

◆ Prepare for frustration when others in a very sequential class, such as math, don't catch on as quickly as you do. You may also become frustrated in discussion classes in which many opinions are expressed and arguments reach an emotional pitch. Learn to let these frustrations roll off your back.

◆ Ask your professor for clear, step-by-step guidelines if instructions are unclear. Also ask if you are not clear on the goal you are expected to achieve with a project.

◆ Ask your professor to fill in gaps if the linear progression of a concept seems to be missing some steps: "How did you get from A to B?"

◆ Categorize information as you take lecture notes.

Study Stressors

Pace yourself in tests, because your natural inclination is to not move on until you've finished a task. Sometimes you must move on to complete the rest of the exam.

Study strategies:

- Study in quiet, well-lit environments.

- Highlight or underline key points in your reading (see Chapter 6).

- Sometimes you have to force yourself to see the big picture. Try not to get too bogged down in details.

- Create outlines, timelines, and diagrams as study aids.

- Turning study materials into puzzles and games will help you learn concepts.

Successful Intelligence

You may know your learning style and how intelligent you are, but how do you use your intelligence to solve problems? Successful Intelligence theory asserts that a person's overall intelligence comprises three distinct elements—analytical, creative, and practical thinking skills.

In his book, *Successful Intelligence* (Simon & Schuster), Robert Sternberg refutes the idea of any one definition of intelligence. Instead, he suggests that successful intelligence determines one's ability to cope in one's career in life—and in school. Successfully intelligent people capitalize on their strengths and recognize and compensate for their weaknesses; self-motivating and flexible in their work style, they create their own opportunities, actively seek out role models, recognize and accurately define problems, and know when to persevere.

Successful intelligence is the kind of intelligence you need to succeed both in school and in the real world. It is the translation of underlying skills and abilities into routines that lead to highly competent everyday performances—on the job, in personal relationships, and in the classroom.

More specifically, Sternberg describes successful intelligence as the ability to balance analytical, practical, and creative intelligence and use these intelligences effectively. And the best news from his more recent work is the affirmation that people can actually perform exercises to improve their three types of thinking.

Analytical intelligence involves the conscious direction of our mental processes to find a thoughtful solution to a problem. It is the ability to overcome obstacles to find a solution. Being analytically intelligent is having the ability to solve problems effectively.

Creative intelligence is the ability to come up with new ideas. With creative intelligence, a person can generate innovative solutions to solve problems.

Practical intelligence is common sense and deals mostly with social situations. Some might refer to this aspect of intelligence as street smarts.

To find out your level of successful intelligence, take the assessment at www.quintcareers.com/intelligence_quiz.html.

How did you do? Which skills do you need to improve? Following are suggestions for improving your thinking skills in each area when solving problems. These suggestions are excellent for working through obstacles you come across in class projects.

Improving Analytical Thinking Skills

- Seek out more (complete) information about the situation/decision.

- Separate the information you do have into fact and opinion.

- Evaluate and decide on the importance of each piece of information.

- Break down larger concepts into smaller, easier-to-manage pieces.

- Dedicate time to gathering, reading, and evaluating information.

A student named Megan Cahoon published an assignment on the Internet describing academic experiences she'd had relating to successful intelligence. She noted that she had encountered analytical thinking skills when she attempted to publish a personal web page but it didn't work. She defined her problem and decided the best course would be to start over. She recreated the page step by step and at each juncture tested whether it would actually work when published on the Internet.

Improving Creative Thinking Skills

- Take risks by pushing yourself out of your comfort zone when seeking understanding.

- Seek out examples of the creative solutions of others to similar situations.

- Examine the situation you face from multiple perspectives.

- Go beyond obvious and conventional solutions.

- Free yourself to brainstorm (develop) multiple solutions to a situation.

Cahoon described encountering her creative thinking skills when she made a paper collage in a class. She detailed the color choices she made and very simple materials she used in making a black cat, the centerpiece of her collage.

Improving Practical Thinking Skills

- Try to observe how others work and make decisions.

- Examine how others have successfully accomplished things.

- Look for patterns in past experience to prepare for future decisions/situations.

- Read and review commonsense tips for everyday situations.

- Apply what you have learned from the past to present day.

Cahoon confronted practical thinking skills in discerning which classmate selected a piece of music that was being played in an activity about nonverbal communication. She looked for patterns in her classmate's nonverbal behavior and used her past knowledge of her classmates to guess who selected the music.

Cahoon also related the three thinking skills to her career goal as a doctor, noting that she would need practical thinking skills to communicate with patients, analytical thinking skills to diagnose them, and creative thinking skills to solve problems in her medical practice.

What You've Learned

Ready for a quick check to see what you've learned from this chapter? I now understand ...

- How to determine my preferred learning style.

- The characteristics of my learning style.

- The ideal classes that suit my learning style.

- The best ways to address my learning style in classroom situations.

- Effective study strategies to suit my learning style.

- How to boost the three aspects of successful intelligence for problem solving.

The Least You Need to Know

- All students have preferred styles of learning but may exhibit multiple and overlapping styles.

- Students won't always be able to choose classes that align with their learning styles, but even when they can't, they can adapt in-class behaviors and study activities to their learning styles.

- Successful intelligence encompasses three types of thinking skills, all of which can be improved upon and employed in solving problems in school and in life.

Chapter **6**

Reading for Comprehension and Memory

In This Chapter

◆ Find out how to determine how much reading to do

◆ Learn to get the most from the entire textbook

◆ Discover ways to be an actively engaged reader

◆ Understand how to remember what you read

Do you fall asleep when trying to read a textbook? One of your authors remembers trying to read chapters of a high-school chemistry text faithfully every Sunday night but *always* falling asleep. Do you find yourself reading the same passage over and over? Do you immediately forget what you've just read? Does your mind wander when you try to read assigned texts? Do you lose concentration or get bored and distracted? Are you a slow reader who spends way too much time on reading assignments?

Do you struggle to afford expensive textbooks? Do you feel it would help you learn better to write in or highlight your textbook, but are afraid to get a poor return on your investment if you try to sell it back with marks in it?

These are all common problems for college readers. This chapter offers strategies not only for confronting these issues, but also for learning to get more out of reading assignments. You'll also get advice on how to understand, remember, and learn what you read, especially so you can succeed on tests and writing assignments drawn from the reading.

How Much and Why

You may be shocked in college to learn exactly how much reading is required. You'll need to read far more than in high school, and you'll need much more advanced reading skills as well. You will likely begin voicing the common student complaint that each professor seems to think his or her class is the only one you have because the magnitude of reading assignments (not to mention all the other assignments) doesn't reflect the fact that you have four or more other classes to prepare for. Many professors assign more than one text—sometimes up to five or more in, for example, literature and seminar-type classes. If you employ the time-management techniques in Chapter 4 and look at how all your reading requirements fit into your schedule, you may even conclude that it is not humanly possible to do all the reading you're expected to do in a semester—especially if you're a slow reader.

Therefore, you need to determine how much and what kind of reading you actually need to do in each class. Virtually all professors assign textbooks or some other kind of reading, but professors don't all use the reading in the same way. You may find that some instructors barely refer to the textbook at all. They may not even test from the reading; instead, grades may be primarily based on discussions, projects, and writing assignments—or tests are based essentially on lecture material. Other professors base everything on reading assignments; the reading is essential to your class preparedness and ability to contribute to discussions, and tests are based entirely on the text. Professors who strongly depend on the text may even teach the reading in class lectures. Somewhere in the middle are professors whose tests combine material from reading and lectures.

Your professor's style of reading usage not only will determine how and how much you read, but also may influence whether you even *buy* the textbook. Textbooks are astonishingly expensive, and their escalating cost has affected students' buying habits and use of texts. Students are often reluctant to buy a book unless it's absolutely necessary. And while most experts recommend either making notes in the text or highlighting, fewer students do so because they want to sell their books back at the end of the semester to recoup some of the huge costs. You must be strategic in planning both reading and purchasing texts.

How can you find out your professor's style of reading usage?

- Ask students who have previously taken the course with the professor.

- Examine the syllabus carefully. Look for the assignment of specific chapters and notations that tests will cover certain chapters. The syllabus may even clarify how essential the textbook is and indicate policies on reading and class preparation.

- Attend a few class sessions at the beginning of the semester *before* you buy the text to see if you can get a feel for how important reading will actually be. (If reading assignments begin right away, see if you can share with a classmate before you buy.) Listen for the professor's emphasis on the reading. Does he or she refer to specific upcoming readings? Does he or she come out and say that a certain item from the text will be on the exam?

- Look at old tests (see Chapter 3) to see the extent to which they are taken from the reading.

- Ask the professor. Be careful about asking because you don't want to convey the impression that you're a slacker who does not intend to do the reading. You might phrase your query something like this: "Buying textbooks is a real financial hardship for me, so I am wondering how much we'll be using the text, and what other options to purchasing may be available." The professor may have an extra copy to lend or would be willing to have a copy placed on reserve in the library. Perhaps you could share a copy with a friend or borrow one from one of the rare students who didn't sell the text back at the end of the semester. Or the professor might tell you not to worry about the text because it won't be used much.

Study Suggestions

Don't let the high cost of textbooks keep you from succeeding in college. You probably already know about buying used copies of texts, but in addition to the preceding ideas for borrowing, sharing, or checking the library for the text, search online for sites that offer substantial discounts on textbooks. Some publishers are making an effort to offer cheaper alternatives, and you may find on a publisher's website, for example, an e-book version of the text available at a lower cost.

Although rarely you can get by without buying or reading the text, be aware that reading is essential to the vast majority of college classes, and professors expect a significant portion of your learning to come from the text. Still, professors' styles of textbook usage can offer clues to how to read:

◆ When you know that the professor heavily uses the text and tests from it, you'll need to do intense, active reading and rereading (discussed later in this chapter).

◆ If the professor teaches from the text, repeating most of the material from the reading, you may have a choice: you can learn the material from class lectures (take good notes, as detailed in Chapter 7), or you can do the reading and let the class lectures reinforce what you've read.

◆ If the professor uses a mix of lecture and reading material on tests, you may be able to get by with skimming the reading (discussed later in this chapter), but until you've taken the first test, it's best to do intense, active reading. After the first test, you may discover you don't need to read as actively and intensely.

Study Suggestions

Remember that no matter how little you can get by with to succeed in a given class, learning should be your goal. If reading will help you learn more in a class that requires minimal reading, try to make time for it.

◆ When the professor uses the reading minimally, you can skim or skip the reading altogether.

Using the Entire Textbook

You will get much more out of college reading if you get acquainted with the many resources that textbooks offer you. Before we get into the ways you can get to know and better use your texts, let's look at some types of texts:

Monograph: A scholarly book on a single subject or a group of related subjects, usually written by one person. Although they're scholarly, many monographs are not written specifically as textbooks. The significance of books not necessarily intended as textbooks is that they usually lack the typical learning aids found in textbooks, such as glossaries, summaries, and questions at the end of chapters.

Sourcebook or reader: A text that may consist of primary sources, secondary sources (see Chapter 11 for more on these types of sources), or a mixture of both. Many are written as textbooks, but some are not.

Literature: For English, composition, and literature classes, you will often read works of literature, such as novels, plays, and books of poetry. Of course, these are not written as textbooks. You may also read literature in foreign language classes, often written in the language you're studying.

Nonstandard texts: These include articles, handouts, web readings, and other texts that fall outside the other categories.

Textbook: A standard textbook is by far the most common type of text you will encounter in your classes. A textbook is often written by multiple authors and is usually a comprehensive and wide-ranging collection of material pertaining to the course. Textbooks are used in every conceivable course: math, science, business, foreign languages, and everything in between.

In addition to assigning various types of textbooks, professors give diverse types of reading assignments. Some reading serves purely as fodder for class discussions or to set up concepts you will learn in class (especially in, say, math and science classes). Other assignments are the core of what you are tested on. Still others are intended to spark writing assignments. Be clear on the purpose for each reading assignment so you can read strategically.

Study Stressors

As if you weren't stressed enough about the required reading, what about the supplemental reading your instructor recommends? While your schedule may not allow you to thoroughly read supplemental assignments, don't overlook them entirely. At least survey them because you could find a gem that will substantially enhance your understanding of course concepts, suggest a paper topic, or give you an extra boost on an essay exam. Also consider talking to your professor about the importance of the supplemental reading.

A significant portion of the research on reading methods focuses on variations of a system called SQ3R, or sometimes SQ4R, which is also mentioned as a general study system in Chapter 8. The SQ3R acronym stands for Survey, Question, Read, Recite, Review. When the fourth R is added, it stands for Record. While we briefly present SQ3R/4R as a reading system worth your consideration, our approach is to integrate elements of SQ3R/4R into the suggestions provided in this chapter.

SQ3R/4R is not the only system to suggest surveying a text before reading it. Surveying, also known as previewing or prereading, is a widely known technique for getting the most out of textbook readings. Experts recommend spending anywhere from 10 minutes to an hour just getting to know the textbook and the many components it offers.

Study Suggestions

Endeavor never to miss class, but especially don't skip class when reading assignments are discussed. You'll get much more out of the reading if you join in the class discussion about it. You may even find that the professor adjusts test questions to reflect what transpired in the class discussions. And, of course, professors love students who participate in class.

At the beginning of a new course, familiarize yourself with these parts of your text:

- **Table of contents**—How is the text organized? Compare the contents to the syllabus reading assignments. Has your professor assigned the chapters in order, or does he or she skip around?

- **Glossary**—Most texts offer a glossary, which can be a major study aid. The glossary will likely contain concepts you'll be tested on.

- **Appendixes**—What's offered in the back of the book? You might find hidden treasures that will help you learn and prepare.

Also ask yourself general questions about the audience for the book and its purpose, especially if it was not written specifically as a textbook.

Before you read each chapter, perform a mini survey of a typical chapter's material:

- **Chapter introduction and conclusion**—These go a long way toward giving you a flavor of the chapter. Look also for a summary of the chapter so you can see the main points.

- **Chapter objectives**—Many texts list what you are expected to learn from the chapter.

- **Overall format and structure of the chapter**—Note how it's organized and what the author does to emphasize key points.

- **Chapter subheadings**—These give you a big-picture view of the chapter's contents.

- **Concepts**—How are concepts handled? You may find them in bold type or defined in the margins.

- **Graphics, photos, illustrations, and tables**—Don't skip these: they can help you understand concepts. Read the captions, too.

- **Sidebars**—These short pieces of supplemental information within the text's chapters may illuminate concepts in the text. You may also find that your professor does not overlook these parts of the reading when preparing tests.

- ◆ **Cases**—Case studies truly help you learn the material because they provide examples of how the concepts are applied in real life. Again, your professor may draw on these in exams.

- ◆ **End-of-chapter material**—Be sure to peruse the back of the chapter. Most texts offer questions about the chapter, usually following the same order as the answers appear in the text. These are wonderful for quizzing yourself, guiding your reading, and ensuring that you understand the chapter.

Now, as you get ready to read an assignment, set yourself up for success by doing the following:

Create an ideal setting: Get comfortable, but not so comfortable that you fall asleep. Minimize distractions, unless you are truly the type who can successfully read with music or even the TV on. The library can be an excellent setting, as can a peaceful outdoor location, weather permitting.

Be sure of the assignment: Review the syllabus or your professor's instructions to make sure you are reading the right material at the right time. Be sure you noted any verbal clues the instructor gave you about the most important aspects of the reading.

Know your concentration span: Determine how long you can concentrate on reading without getting bored or distracted. Most college students can't last much longer than about 50 minutes, while some lose focus after a considerably shorter period. Know what works for you because you will just waste time if you try to read beyond your concentration span.

Set a goal: Based on your concentration span, decide how much time you will devote to a given reading assignment in one sitting. You can base your goal on a certain time period, a number of chapters, or a span of pages. Factor in your concentration span so you can read for that span and then take a break. For example, decide that you will read for two hours with a 10-minute break in the middle. Or calculate the number of pages you need to read, divide them by the number of time segments you want to devote to one sitting, and take breaks after every X number of pages.

Active Reading for Understanding

It's natural to simply read a chapter from beginning to end, but it's not the most effective way to read, learn, and understand the content you're reading.

Most experts recommend active or critical reading. If you're not doing something to be actively engaged in your reading, you will probably find that you have to reread before the test, maybe even multiple times. You won't learn or retain much if you simply read.

The vast majority of experts recommend annotating your textbooks as the best form of active reading—in other words, making notes in the margins. We've already pointed out why that suggestion is a problem for many college students; textbooks are extremely expensive, and students want to sell them back. Because annotating is so highly recommended, we offer some suggestions for the textbook issue:

◆ Seriously consider *not* selling your textbooks. Yes, it's a huge sacrifice not to recoup your huge investment in textbooks, but it may pay off in better grades. You might also consider trying to sell your books privately to other students or through an online auction site instead of at your campus bookstore. You may get more value for a marked-up book through those venues than through the bookstore.

◆ Annotate in pencil that you can erase at the end of the semester. Keep in mind, however, that even erased pencil will dramatically lower the book's value at buyback time.

◆ Look into the availability of an e-book version of the text that you can download, print, and annotate to your heart's content. Also look at sites like www.ichapters.com for e-books and chapters.

◆ See the next section, which suggests taking notes outside the textbook.

What exactly do you write when you annotate? To some extent, the content of your annotations isn't as important as the active engagement of writing the notes. However, here are some suggestions:

◆ Thoughts on connections between this book and others you've read, both in this course and outside of it

◆ Restatements in your own words of the thesis statement of each paragraph or section

◆ Definitions of unfamiliar words

◆ Your own system of symbols to mark important passages, such as exclamation points (!) for key points and question marks (?) for points you have questions about

◆ Comments of agreement or disagreement with ideas in the text

◆ Your own ideas inspired by the text

◆ Other examples of concepts discussed in the text

The second-most highly recommended system for actively engaging with reading is highlighting, which, of course, comes with the same textbook-buyback problem that annotating does. Highlighting can also be less effective than annotating because students tend to highlight way too much of the text. Learn to be selective and discriminating when you highlight; otherwise, the important points won't stand out. Scholars recommend highlighting as little as 10 to 15 percent of a page and as much as 50 percent—but certainly no more than that. If you tend to highlight toward the higher end of that range, at least try this visualization: imagine that the words on the page are flowing into your highlighter and through your arm, into your neck, and into your brain. Surveying the chapters can also help you to be a more discriminating highlighter. Once you preview what's in a chapter, you have a much better idea of what's important enough to be highlighted.

You can also actively engage with the assigned reading by synthesizing your textbook reading with lecture notes you've taken in class. Try to integrate your notes from both sources into a "big picture" perspective. Compare the reading with class notes. What are the areas of agreement and disagreement? Where are the gaps? What part of the reading did your professor stress in lectures? This approach is especially helpful when you know that the teacher places equal emphasis in tests on the reading and class lectures.

When the main objective of a reading assignment is a written response or writing assignment about it, two effective techniques for actively engaging in the reading are brainstorming and freewriting.

Brainstorming, covered in detail in Chapter 11, entails making a list of everything you can think of about the reading and your reaction to it. What do you already know about this topic? How do you feel about it? What is new for you? This brainstormed list can be a jumping-off point for a paper about the assigned reading.

The idea behind freewriting is to just sit down and write for 15 minutes straight. The first step is closely akin to brainstorming. Write down as many thoughts about the reading as you can, but instead of putting them down in a list format, write them roughly in the form of sentences and paragraphs. Pay no attention to writing correctly, and don't go back to make revisions. Simply endeavor to get as many words down about the reading as possible within a period of about 15 minutes, trying not to pause. The resulting piece of writing most likely will be a throwaway, but it might contain some good ideas that you can use in the piece of writing assigned about the reading.

Reading techniques vary a bit by subject. Here are a few tips for reading texts in specialized areas:

Math: Read the text in order because math competency builds on what you've already learned. Pay attention to illustrations. Make notes of formulas, proofs, theorems, definitions, and the like. Note cards are great for this purpose. Work as many sample problems as you can, even if they're not assigned as homework. Allot extra time for reading a math book if you are not strong in math.

History: Look for timelines and summaries of important events. Make particular note of causes of historical occurrences, as well as their outcomes. Does the author present competing interpretations for these causes and effects? See if the reading conveys a feel for the historical period it discusses. Try to discern the social context of the period. Practice comparing various historical periods. Pay special attention to maps and illustrations.

Literature: Devote particular attention to the six standard elements of novels and stories: characters, setting, time, problem or conflict, events, and solution or resolution.

Advanced Active Reading to Learn Key Concepts

To become even more actively engaged in your reading and to enhance your learning of key terms, you can employ techniques of questioning, outlining, and note taking. In this section, we integrate the Q (Question) and first R (Read) of the SQ3R/4R method. Consider these more advanced techniques for engaging with your reading:

Ask questions: As you are completing an assigned reading, make up questions to ask yourself about the reading and answer them as you read. Asking and answering questions is a proven way to cement the reading in your mind. If you're wondering how to go about making up questions, try these methods:

◆ Use the questions that journalists answer in newspaper stories: who, what, where, when, why, and how. As you come to a concept in the text, determine which of these questions best applies and then answer it through your reading. Examples: Who is Aeneas, the protagonist of Latin poet Vergil's epic poem, *The Aeneid?* What do snakes symbolize in *The Aeneid?* Where was Queen Dido's kingdom? When does *The Aeneid* take place? Why do the pagan gods play certain roles in *The Aeneid?* How does *The Aeneid* compare with Homer's *Odyssey?*

◆ Rephrase chapter headings as questions.

◆ Put yourself in your professor's place and ask yourself, "What questions would my professor ask about this reading if making up a test?"

◆ As mentioned, use the questions in the back of each chapter.

If you'd like to learn more about the SQ3R/4R reading method and consider implementing it, check out these websites:

◆ www.kishwaukeecollege.edu/learning_skills_center/ study_skills_help/read_textbook.shtml

◆ http://academic.cuesta.edu/acasupp/AS/306.HTM

Other techniques include these:

◆ **P2R (also called PRR)**—A shortened version of SQ3R/4R that includes Preview, Read, Review/Recall. See www.utexas.edu/ student/utlc/lrnres/handouts/reading/prr.pdf.

◆ **REDW**—We recommend this method (which stands for Read, Examine, Decide, Write) only for short readings because it is very time-consuming. See http://studyskills6.wikispaces.com/REDW.

Take notes: Writing down notes on your reading in a place other than the textbook itself is a way to solve the textbook buyback problem. You can take notes in a notebook, on loose-leaf paper, on a legal pad, or on note cards (the method we recommend). Writing reading notes on 3×5 index cards is a highly effective method because you can, for example, write a concept on one side of the card and a definition on the back, or a question on one side and the answer on the back. You can then use the cards to test yourself as a highly portable study method (see also Chapter 8).

Summarize: If you can summarize the main ideas of a section in a chapter, that's a pretty good indication that you have actively engaged in the reading and absorbed the concepts. You can try writing your summaries on your note cards or other medium you're using for notes. If you can't summarize a section without looking back at it, you may need to read it again.

Use sticky notes: Another terrific way to address the textbook buy-back issue is to take notes on sticky notes. These are an excellent compromise between writing inside your text and making notes outside because the notes will be in the book, but the pages won't be marked. The only downside is that you may use a lot of sticky notes and rack up a bit of expense. Use them to mark important pages, and on the sticky note, write the major topic of the page. Then use smaller notes to mark important passages and write your own notes and questions. Sticky notes are also fantastic for open-book tests because they can help you locate information quickly.

Study Stories

"The only way I found to absorb a dense textbook was to invert it. By that, I mean I'd take a notebook and devote a page to every proper name, number, date, or concept I came across. It's not enough to read a textbook. You've got to reorganize it mentally in a way that demands enough thought to make it stick in the brain. This method is a simple mechanism for forcing you to do exactly that."

—David C., commenting on a blog entry at Lifehack.org

Outline: You may want to develop your notes into an outline. Outlining chapters is a time-honored way to engage with and really dissect the reading. Some experts suggest that outlining is the smart way to take notes because the outline structure enables you to be selective and not repeat the entire text in your notes. To outline, write down the subheadings and the main topic of each paragraph.

No matter which advanced technique you choose for engaging actively with your reading assignments, be sure to look up unfamiliar words as you read. See if your textbook has a glossary, but also keep a dictionary handy for words that aren't in the glossary or texts that don't have a glossary.

Study Stories

"I read the material and outline it so that I can read over my notes a couple of times before the exam. There are very few people who can read a textbook and retain all the detailed information they read, and I'm not one of them. I have to put in the time, but it always pays off."

—Jessica H.

Occasionally, you may find yourself in a "reading emergency," meaning you have a test scheduled and you have not done the reading. If you find yourself in this position, try skimming, which entails reading the chapter's introduction and conclusion. Read all chapter subheadings and the first and last paragraph of each section. Identify the main ideas in each paragraph.

Also consider obtaining book summaries, free study guides and summaries of books online (with more elaborate study aids available for a price), from Cliffs Notes (www.cliffsnotes.com) and Pink Monkey (www.pinkmonkey.com). Use these only in a pinch, and be aware that the book summaries primarily cover literature. Other subjects are covered but aren't geared to particular textbooks. And you still have to do *some* reading.

Methods for Improving Memory

The preceding methods will help you engage actively with your reading assignments and learn, but to truly remember what you read and save yourself time when studying, add even more power to your reading techniques with tricks that align with the Record, Recite, and Review steps of the SQ3R/4R system. Here's how to kick your reading and memory of your reading into high gear:

Reread: The more you read your assignments, the more you will remember them. Some experts suggest reading a chapter twice and then reading it again before a test. While this technique is definitely effective, it is time-consuming, especially if you read slowly. It's more efficient to reread chapter subheadings and key passages (such as passages you've highlighted or annotated), or reread the notes you've taken outside the text, such as on note cards.

Make your own study guide: An extension of the concept of composing questions about your reading, this technique involves creating a set of possible test questions and answers and studying from those. Determine what your professor is likely to ask, compose questions, and write the answers under them. Study from your study guide until you feel you know it well. Then create a version that omits the answers and see how well you do answering the questions. Those you miss are the ones you need to study more.

Use note cards as flash cards: If you chose to take notes on cards, you can now use those as flash cards to test your memory of the reading. See Chapter 8 for more information on using flash cards.

Use Cornell Notes: This technique, detailed in Chapter 7, is more commonly used for taking lecture notes but can also be used to take reading notes. You can learn more about the system at http://academic. cuesta.edu/acasupp/as/619.htm and see a sample setup for a page of notes at www.clt.cornell.edu/campus/learn/LSC%20Resources/ cornellsystem.pdf.

Study Stressors _____

Think you can remember aspects of your reading by repeating them over and over again? Sure you can—for a brief period. Repeating information may get you through a test, but you won't retain the information. You'll have to relearn it, which especially wastes time if you have a cumulative final exam. You also defeat the purpose of learning if you don't retain the material beyond the test.

Recite and teach material to others: Many experts swear by the effectiveness of reciting important parts of the reading orally—not reading aloud, but reciting section summaries you've composed yourself or questions and answers you've posed about the reading. Since you might find it awkward to recite aloud with people around, you may want to find a private place. In the same vein, teaching the material to others can dramatically boost your memory of it. Study groups are an excellent setting for doing so. If all else fails, consider teaching concepts to your dog or one of your stuffed animals.

Consider improving your reading speed: While it may seem strange to discuss increasing reading speed in this section, studies show that reading faster actually boosts comprehension and memory. You'd think that the opposite would be true—that you'd comprehend more if you slow down and take your time—but it's not, because you tend to lose concentration when you read slowly. Not everyone is comfortable with a faster reading speed. It takes some getting used to, but if you find that slow reading is making it impossible for you to complete all your reading assignments, you should be able to find a speed-reading course at your college, nearby, or even through the Internet. You can find a good resource on the basics of faster reading at www.uwgb.edu/ tutoring/resources/rapid.asp. For an interesting narrative of English professor Richard Jewell's experience with learning to read faster in graduate school, go here: www.tc.umn.edu/~jewel001/CollegeWriting/ READSPEAKTHINK/READ/HowToRead.htm#Speed.

Visualize: As you come across a concept in your reading, make a mental picture of it. For example, if you will be tested on human digestion, visualize the digestive process in your mind. Everyone visualizes to a certain extent, but to commit a concept to memory, really concentrate and create a detailed mental picture.

Draw concepts: The next step beyond visualizing is to draw pictures of concepts. This technique will especially help you if you are a visual learner (see Chapter 5).

What You've Learned

Ready for a quick check to see what you've learned from this chapter? I now understand ...

◆ How to evaluate how much reading I need to do to succeed.

◆ Tricks for dealing with the high cost of textbooks and the problem of selling back texts I've written in.

◆ Ways to use textbooks as comprehensive learning tools.

◆ The secret of being an active reader for greater comprehension and learning.

◆ How to remember more of what I read and reduce study time.

The Least You Need to Know

◆ Although college students face high textbook costs and more reading requirements than they ever did in high school, they can succeed with college reading.

◆ Students must create an environment and strategy that is most conducive to effective reading.

◆ Developing a personal system that promotes active engagement with the reading is a crucial key to comprehension, retention, and memorization.

Part 3

Establishing Success in the Classroom

Some of the keys to better grades involve preparation, studying, and test taking.

The following chapters guide you in developing critical strategies for classroom preparation, reviewing and creating a study method that works for you, and understanding the ins and outs of various testing methods. Also included is a chapter on study tips for specific subjects that often require extra effort.

Chapter 7

Class Preparation and Note Taking

In This Chapter

- ◆ Learn the ins and outs of preparing for classes
- ◆ Develop active listening and learning skills
- ◆ Realize the importance of knowing your professor
- ◆ Understand why and how to take great class notes

We begin this part of the book with a chapter on one of the most important elements to becoming a strategic learner and learning your course material: the classroom.

What happens in the classroom (and sometimes outside it) has a major impact on whether you'll truly understand the subject. This will most certainly have a direct impact on your academic performance.

This chapter focuses on several key elements of succeeding in the classroom, including understanding what's required of you, knowing your professor, listening and learning actively, participating in class, and taking good notes.

Using the Syllabus and Course Calendar

One of the hardest lessons to learn about college is that, unlike many of the previous 12 years you've been in school, college professors expect you to be prepared for every class without having to do the constant reminders that your teachers used to do. You won't see little notes on the board to remind you of upcoming papers, quizzes, or tests. You're expected to know the course syllabus and calendar, and plan accordingly.

You may already know the answer, but what is a course syllabus? While it's traditionally a printed document outlining the course that professors distribute on the first day of classes, more professors are now posting the syllabus online for students to view at their leisure. At its most basic, a syllabus is an overview or outline of the course, along with a schedule of topics that will be covered. But seasoned students know they can glean a wealth of information from it, including detailed information on all the graded assignments, what is generally expected of students to pass the course, and how the course will be run.

You'll want to carefully read and reread the syllabus for every course you take. Both faculty and students often refer to a course syllabus as the contract between instructor and student—one that lasts from the first day of class until the last. Instructors view the syllabus as the final word on any grading or policy dispute with a student, and they expect all students to have thoroughly read it by the first week of classes. Students see the syllabus as a tool that can protect them if the professor veers off course or attempts to change major course requirements or grading policies.

Study Stressors _____

Whatever you do, don't be that student who constantly asks professors questions about the course that could easily be answered by reviewing the syllabus. Students who ask these obvious questions are immediately labeled by faculty as students who don't care about the class. Instructors spend a lot of time and effort to develop the course syllabus; it's seen as kind of a slap in the face to ignore their efforts by not reading and knowing the syllabus.

Here are the key components of a syllabus:

♦ **Course essentials**—Includes the course title, number, and credits; the classroom location; and the time and days of the week the class is offered.

♦ **Instructor information**—Supplies the name of the instructor and his or her office location, office hours, phone, and e-mail.

♦ **Required reading**—Provides a list of textbooks, reading packets, and any other reading materials required for the course.

♦ **Supplemental reading**—Lists additional reading materials that students are not required to read but that they may find helpful in understanding the course material.

♦ **Course overview**—Offers a general overview of the course, often taken directly from the college catalog description. Some professors create their own course overview loosely based on the catalog description.

Study Stories

"I think one of the most important things to do during the first week of classes is to read—and I mean really read—the syllabus from each course I'm taking. What I do is highlight the most important stuff about papers, projects, and stuff. Then I go to the calendar section and transfer all the important due dates to my personal planner. That way, at any time, I can look at my planner and know what assignments are coming due in all of my classes."

—Jill S.

♦ **Course expectations**—Explains what students should expect from the class, including the teaching method used (lecture, discussion, lab, and so on), the role of the student, and an overview of the class.

♦ **Learning objectives**—Describes what students are expected to learn by completing the course.

♦ **Course requirements**—Provides details about the key graded assignments and the evaluation methods for grading them.

- ◆ **Course policies**—Includes information on student attendance (and whether it counts toward your grade), class participation, missed classes/assignments, make-up policies, academic honesty, and classroom policies.

- ◆ **Course calendar**—Lists a day-by-day or weekly schedule of reading assignments, tests, and other graded assignments for the course.

Knowing Your Professor

Over the course of your college career, you'll spend at least 1,800 hours listening to your professors lecture, lead discussions, or otherwise facilitate learning in the classroom.

With all that time spent in the classroom, you might think you would know your professors, but you won't. While it is certainly important to use class time wisely (see the next few sections), it's just as important to use time outside of class to get to know your professors better. More important, this will give your professors a chance to get to know you better.

Study Suggestions _____

The Halo Effect is a benefit that you can directly derive from visiting with your professors in their offices. The Halo Effect is a theory that your performance in one area affects how a professor will grade you in another. In other words, if you perform well on your first assignment, the professor may be inclined to similarly grade your other work in the class. The same idea holds true if the professor knows you and likes you and believes that you are trying your best in the class, which he or she would know only by your visits to the office.

Getting to know your professors will be very rewarding to you—both in the short run and in the longer term. For example, here are the major benefits of knowing your professors—and being known by them:

- ◆ **Deeper understanding of course material**—One of the biggest benefits is simply getting answers to questions you have about the course content.

◆ **Insights into graded assignments**—Often a professor will share more information about some of the key graded assignments for the class, providing you with valuable insider information that should improve your performance.

◆ **Additional motivation to succeed**—It can also add a little stress, but encouragement from your professor to dig deeper and complete additional readings can greatly enhance your knowledge of a subject.

◆ **Improvement in your grades**—When professors know your attitude and work ethic and see that you are trying to succeed, they will often grade you a bit more leniently from others. Read more about this in the earlier sidebar on the Halo Effect.

◆ **Career and life advice**—Professors are good sources for information about majors, minors, careers, internships, and graduate schools. Take the time to pick their brains to help with your future plans and goals.

◆ **Support for future endeavors**—You're very likely to need a letter of recommendation or nomination for scholarships, awards, internships, or graduate studies. You're much more likely to receive a strong show of support from professors who know you.

> **Study Stories**
>
> "Whether you are at a big or small school, make every effort to be friends with your professors. Get them to know you. Not only will it help you get through class or make a higher letter grade, but after graduation, they can help you find jobs, give you advice on life, and just be there for you."
>
> —Laura W.

◆ **A professional network**—One of the most powerful tools you'll use in your lifetime is your network of contacts—and your professors often have key contacts in their profession who can assist you in myriad ways.

◆ **A mentoring relationship**—If you're lucky, you'll leave college with at least one professor with whom you have a close mentoring relationship that will last long after you graduate.

Study Stressors

What happens if you finally get up the courage to see your professor and he or she is not in the office? Whatever you do, do not confront the professor about not being available during office hours. One of the biggest pet peeves we hear from professors—and one that immediately puts you in a hole—is when students accuse them of skipping office hours. Instead of saying "I came by your office and you were not there during your office hours," state "I must have just missed you during your office hours and would like to schedule an appointment to talk."

Can it be intimidating walking into a professor's office for the first time? Of course it can—and with some professors, it's much more intimidating than others! Faculty generally like to talk with students, whether to allay fears, explain assignments in more depth, or discuss additional readings. What do you do if you're too afraid to make your first chat with the professor in his or her office? Try to catch him or her right after class and break the ice with a simple introduction or question. Once you've made that initial contact, follow up with a visit to the office. One final hint: always address the professor by his or her proper title (Dr., Mr., Ms., or Professor) and know how to pronounce his or her name.

Active Listening and Learning

There's a theory that the more you listen, the more you learn. The theory, called *learning to listen—listening to learn*, is about developing the skill and effort to listen effectively. Students may hear a class lecture, but if they are not actively thinking about what is being said, they will not absorb much of the spoken material. If you want to benefit from showing up to class and attending the lecture, you'll need to work at actively listening to the instructor.

Typically, when you enroll in a class, it's because you want to take it, but sometimes, of course, required classes may not appeal to you. Or maybe it's a class taught by a really boring professor. Whatever the situation, it's important to not only show up for your classes, but to show up and be prepared to actively listen and learn. By actively listening, you are purposely focusing on the instructor so that you can fully understand what he or she is communicating.

Several class-related factors can affect your active listening abilities. You'll need to overcome these if you want to learn the material.

◆ **Interest in the subject**—The more complex the subject, and the less you are interested in it, the harder you'll have to work at being actively engaged.

◆ **Abilities of the instructor**—Numerous factors related to the instructor's ability to present the material affect your ability to actively listen. For example, your professor might speak too slowly or too quickly, might be too soft-spoken, or might read directly from lecture notes or the text- book.

Study Suggestions

One of the best strate- gies for getting into the habit of active listening and learning is to sit in one of the first rows of the class. Numerous studies show a correlation between where you sit in class and the grade you receive: those who sit in the front of the class are more likely to receive better grades.

◆ **Presentation style**—Some instructors are much better about presenting material in a logical order, or even outlining their presenta- tions. The more haphazard you find the presentation, the harder you'll have to work at listening.

◆ **Classroom environment**—Things such as temperature, noisy students, and noises from outside the classroom can all affect your ability to actively listen.

Study Suggestions

Even if you don't currently have the best listening skills, you can train yourself to be better—and then make it a habit to use those skills in your classes. Active listening is about intensely focusing on listening to the person who is speaking in order to better understand what he or she is saying—not just with your ears, but also with your eyes and other senses.

Here are some tips for dealing with personal factors that can affect your active listening abilities:

- **Arrive prepared**—If you've done the reading assignment, you'll be better able to grasp the instructor's words.

- **Have a positive attitude**—It's easier for classes you like, but it's even more important for classes in which you do not have a strong emotional investment.

- **Leave emotional baggage at the door**—As best you can, put any emotional stressors on hold when you enter class. Otherwise, all you'll remember from the class is what was bothering you.

- **Avoid being inside your head**—Often when you disagree with the subject matter, you start having a mock argument in your head. Put aside any negative opinions and focus on the content being discussed.

- **Focus your attention on the professor**—Don't talk to the student next to you, surf the web, read the student newspaper, or text a friend.

- **Take good notes**—Focusing on taking good notes strengthens your listening skills—just don't try to write down every word your professor says. (Review our note-taking suggestions later in this chapter.)

Participating in Class

You'll find it easier to participate in some classes more than others, but if you make it a goal to ask and answer questions, you'll understand the course material better, become known by the instructor, and earn better grades. Plus, class discussion can break up a somewhat boring lecture style, take discussion down an unpredictable path, and energize both instructor and students alike. Class participation makes the class more stimulating and interesting to both students and faculty.

Study Suggestions

If you take nothing else from this book, we hope you take this advice to heart. Professors love students who contribute to class discussions, so find a way you can participate in your classes. The most common way, of course, is to ask or answer questions in class. You can also chat with professors before or after class, or phone or e-mail them.

But participating in class is easier said than done at times. In many classes, for example, only a handful of students participate. Why don't more students participate in class discussions? See if you've used one of these excuses in the past for not participating:

- ◆ **You fear being incorrect or being perceived as a weak student.** Most instructors don't judge your answers as much as your attempt to answer the question. And certainly when the question is simply asking your opinion, there is no right or wrong response.

- ◆ **Peer pressure prompts you to avoid being seen as a "teacher's pet."** In smaller schools, this issue might be harder to overcome, but you should be more concerned about how your professor sees you than how your classmates do.

- ◆ **A handful of students dominate discussion.** Professors like to have more students engaged in the conversation. Even if a few dominate, raise your hand or attempt to enter the conversation; the instructor will often ask you to join in.

- ◆ **You're shy and don't like speaking in public.** While you may be uncomfortable speaking in front of others, the classroom is the best environment for overcoming a fear that you'll need to overcome to be successful in life.

- ◆ **The course subject is of little interest to you.** You should always be able to

Study Stressors

Participating in class is wonderful. Just do not become that student who never stops talking, asks questions that are way off topic, talks to a friend rather than participating in class, and otherwise becomes a nuisance to the class and the instructor.

find something in your classes that sparks your interest enough to talk about it in class.

Here are some tips for participating in class:

♦ Overcome any fears by convincing yourself that everyone has the right to his or her ideas and opinions.

♦ Organize your thoughts before just blurting out a question or a response to a question.

♦ Take your time, but try to keep your thoughts brief and to the point. Avoid rambling.

♦ Don't interrupt others when they are talking—and respect their opinion. (This is sort of the "golden rule" of class participation.)

♦ Use your text or other readings to support your argument, but don't read large passages to do so.

> **Study Stories**
>
> "Go to every class. I think if you just show up to every class, it will make a big difference in your grades and your performance. That is half the battle and is what I try to do every semester."
>
> —Sabrina O.

♦ Try to avoid arguing a point from an emotional standpoint.

♦ Don't preface your observations with unnecessary comments, such as "This is just my opinion." (Of course it's your opinion.)

♦ Just do it!

Note Taking

One of the most important skills to learn is how to take good class notes. Taking notes will keep you actively engaged in the course material, help organize your thinking and opinions on the material, and better prepare you for studying for quizzes and exams.

We discuss five well-accepted note-taking methods in this section, but before we get to them, here are five general tips for taking good notes:

◆ Don't try to write notes verbatim. Listen to what the professor is saying and then write down the main points. Writing down the material is extremely important, but listening and analyzing while doing so is just as important.

◆ Pay attention to cues. Some professors will actually lecture from an outline, making it easy for students to capture the key information. For others, look for verbal or nonverbal cues, such as pausing for emphasis, restating a point, or changing tone of voice as a signal of a topic shift.

> **Study Stories**
>
> "I love notes. Although I would read the textbooks, my notes are what got me through my classes. If you can become an amazing note-taker, then you will be great. Just stay organized; learn shorthand; and if you have a gap, look it up or ask the professor to help you out."
>
> —Laura W.

◆ Focus on the major points and key arguments. Don't get lost in trying to record all the minor details or examples. Instead, use the time to make sure you understand the key details, formulas, and facts.

◆ Develop some sort of system for abbreviations to keep from getting too caught up in taking notes and not enough in listening. Legibility is also important here, so be sure you understand your own system!

◆ Pay attention to details. Material that is presented in a PowerPoint presentation, shown on a document camera, pulled from a website, or written on the board typically is important information you should have in your notes.

Here's a short description of the commonly accepted note-taking techniques. As with all the advice in this book, use the parts that make sense to make your own note-taking system.

◆ **The Charting Method**—This technique takes preparation before class. In this method, you make several columns on a piece of paper, each one representing an important category of information you expect to be covered in the lecture (based on your reading of the appropriate chapter in the textbook). The Charting Method typically works best for basic classes in which the lectures contain many facts, dates, and relationships. The advantage of this method is that it puts the entire content of a lecture on one page of notes. The disadvantage is that you need to be prepared beforehand to make it work.

◆ **The Cornell Method**—This technique involves dividing your notepaper into two columns: a 2½-inch left column/margin and a 6-inch right column. During class, take notes in the right column, leaving a few lines between major points. Once class is over, add as much detail to your notes as possible. Then, in the left column, write short descriptions, keywords, or questions that relate to the key points in the right column. Using this method allows you to have a column of key concepts and ideas, along with a detailed explanation of each in the other column. Leave some space at the bottom of each page to write a short sentence summarizing the notes on the page.

Study Stories

"When I'm taking notes in a class that is mostly lecture, I write down the topic we are on and then make bullet points underneath. I just write down the main points; if you try to write down everything that the professor is saying, then you are certain to miss something important that is being said while you are trying to write. For these types of classes, I usually go back through my notes shortly after class and fill in other points that I remember while the lecture is still fresh in my mind. You can also go to the book and make extra notes on the topics that you feel you need to. When the professor uses an example to explain something, I put 'ex: (keyword that will remind me of the example)' in my notes. This way, I don't have to write down the entire example—I just have a keyword that will trigger my memory. In classes that post PowerPoint slides before the class, I like to print them in notes view and take them to class with me so I can really listen to the professor and take additional notes as needed next to the slides."

—Cayla C.

◆ **The Mapping Method**—This technique is all about relating facts from lectures to each other in some form of graphic representation (such as tree diagrams), typically revolving around the central point(s) of the lecture. This method works well for when you have lectures that cover large amounts of interrelated material. Because you are connecting concepts as they are discussed, this method also fosters active learning and critical thinking. (Mapping is also an excellent tool for studying and organizing papers.)

◆ **The Outlining Method**—This technique is probably the most common and natural of all the note-taking methods. It involves listening to the lecture/discussion and writing key points and material in a logical pattern or order. Because many lectures are presented in outline form, this method works naturally in those classes. As with any outline method, your notes should be organized around major points, followed by supporting information (either indented or bulleted). Your notes will be extremely well organized and include great detail, but if the instructor speaks too quickly or you get caught up in trying to capture one point, you may not be able to capture all the lecture content.

◆ **The Sentence Method**—This technique is the best note-taking method when speed and efficiency are the crucial elements. In this method, typically when the instructor covers a large amount of material in a short period of time, you simply write each new fact, definition, or topic on a separate line of your notebook. While it works well for capturing large amounts of information, this technique does not allow you to capture relationships or identify major points from minor points. If you use this method, you'll want to spend time after the lecture making the key connections and summarizing major points.

Here are a few important note-taking do's and don'ts:

◆ Do read the assigned readings for class ahead of time, perhaps even taking some preliminary notes for class lecture.

◆ Don't sit next to your friends in class if you are looking to take good notes.

- Don't hesitate to ask questions of the professor if you don't understand something.

- Do attempt to capture in your notes main ideas, key facts, vocabulary, and critical examples.

- Don't doodle or otherwise disengage from taking notes.

What You've Learned

Ready for a quick check to see what you've learned from this chapter? I now understand ...

- It's important to thoroughly review the syllabus for each class.

- I should get to know my professors—and help them get to know me, too.

- I should better prepare myself to actively listen and learn in every class.

- Participating in class discussion is important.

- I need to develop my own system of taking good class notes.

The Least You Need to Know

- Success in the classroom comes from much more than simply showing up for class every day.

- Professors can play a big role in future successes—and can help in many ways beyond simply teaching.

- The most successful students are those who actively engage in the classroom by listening, participating, and taking good notes.

- A key to learning more in classes involves some preparation before each class—as well as careful review afterward.

Chapter 8

Study Tools

In This Chapter

- ◆ Learn about several valuable study tools
- ◆ Build your inventory of active study strategies
- ◆ Develop a productive study pattern for success

Previous chapters have already given you a lot of great tools for helping you achieve greater academic success. This chapter gets into the nitty-gritty of studying and preparing for quizzes and exams.

Our goal with this chapter is to provide you with an overview of the most crucial study tools that top students use to prepare for exams, along with our keen insights. This chapter is not meant to be an exhaustive review of all types of study aids—just the ones we feel are the best for you to consider using.

As you move forward toward becoming a strategic learner and achieving better grades, consider adding some of these key study tools to your arsenal. Remember that your objective with any study tool is to learn one of two types of information: the specific details (such as vocabulary, dates, formulas) or the big picture (frameworks, processes, overall meaning of content).

One final note before we begin: these study tools are all focused on helping you learn, not just memorize. What's the difference? Memorization is short term, meaning what you memorize today will begin to fade pretty quickly. Learning is long term because it transfers what you are studying into something that you can apply to various situations. And the more you use something, the longer you retain it.

Study Systems

Plenty of study systems have been developed over the years. If you're struggling academically, one of these systems can be the beginning of the process that moves you forward toward better grades. Our goal with this section of the chapter is to provide you a brief overview and critique of the major study systems. If you seek more information about any one of them, you'll find links to more information in the appendix.

One common theme to all of these approaches is that they require something more than simply reviewing and rereading your notes. These systems all require you to actively do something—to engage your brain in a deeper way of thinking about the material you are studying. Just remember not to spend so much time preparing for the test that you forget to actually study for it and advance your understanding of the material.

Study Suggestions

Learning these study tools won't really help you much if you have concentration issues—problems with focusing your thinking on what you're doing. Take the time to identify things that distract you when studying. Some common distracters include poor lighting, people's voices, loud noises, the television, e-mail/IMs/texts, temperature issues, lack of motivation, hunger, stress, negative feelings/self-talk, and a cluttered or uncomfortable workspace.

One final note about these study systems: remember that no one magic system will make you a better student. Becoming a better student has to be your personal mission. Remember, too, that as you use one of these systems or develop your own, your learning style (see Chapter 5) should play a key role. Finally, as we've said previously, you should feel free to take parts of these systems that work for you and discard the parts that don't.

Study Stressors

Don't confuse simply adding more time to your studying time with actively studying. An underlying point of this book is that you can learn to study smarter without necessarily studying longer. But even if you have to commit more time to your studying, use that time wisely. Don't waste your time on "prestudy" techniques, such as organizing and reorganizing your notes, completing detailed outlines of the chapters, or color-coding all your study materials. Spend all your time and energy on activities that advance your learning of the material.

Here are the major study systems, along with a short description of each of them.

A.S.P.I.R.E., which stands for the words *approach, select, piece together, investigate, reflect,* and *evaluate. Approach* deals with having a positive attitude, avoiding distractions, and making time in your schedule for studying. *Select* is about studying in reasonable time chunks, deciding on key materials to review, and marking any information you don't understand. *Piece together* relates to synthesizing and summarizing the material you're studying, either by yourself or with a study partner. *Investigate* has you go out and find alternative sources for the information you don't understand. *Reflect* focuses on applying the concepts you're learning, to make them more interesting and easier to remember. *Evaluate* centers on examining your performance on quizzes and tests, detecting a pattern for your errors, and exploring ways to fix your mistakes for future examinations.

Mind-mapping, which is a great tool for courses with a vast amount of interrelated information, helps you to recall an entire section's content from a single term. Mind maps allow you to see the relative importance of course concepts and the way in which the concepts relate to one another. Mind maps are created around a central word, idea, or theme. From this central word, you create branches to other major concepts related to the central word. From there, you continue to create branches from every word or concept you add to the map—and keep doing so until you have all the material on your map. By focusing on key concepts that you discover and define, and then looking for branches and connections among all the concepts, you are mapping knowledge in a way that will help you better understand and remember the information. This approach is sometimes referred to as *concept mapping.*

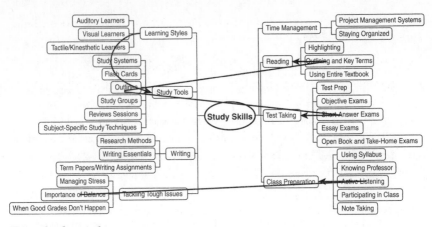

Example of a mind map.

Study Stories

"In high school, teachers assign lots of 'check-up' assignments to make sure you understand the material—through things like homework, quizzes, and practice tests. In college, professors expect you to do these things on your own, without being told to. I had to really figure out what worked and what didn't study-wise in college on my own, because I really didn't have a study method in high school. By the time the tests came around, I'd been working on the material so much that I pretty much didn't need to additionally prepare for it. When I got to college, I realized that after a professor was done talking about a subject, they moved on ... no rehashing the subject, no check-up assignments, nothing. That was my job!"

—Jessica W.

Mnemonics involves organizing key concepts in such a way, using each concept's first letter to create a sense or nonsense word or acronym that you can easily remember. Originating from the Greek term for "memory," mnemonics is an effective way to remember hard-to-retain lists of facts. For example, if you were trying to remember the order of taxonomy in biology, you might use a common mnemonic (or make one of your own), such as *Kids Prefer Cheese Over Fresh Garden Salad*, which is designed to help recall Kingdom, Phylum, Class, Order, Family, Genus, Species. Instead of using words and sentences, you can also simply create a word or phrases with the letters of each item—for example,

Roy G Biv for the colors of a rainbow: red, orange, yellow, green, blue, indigo, and violet.

M.U.R.D.E.R., which stands for the words *mood, understand, recall, digest, expand,* and *review,* is a fairly basic system, which is especially good if you're new to studying. *Mood* deals with having the right attitude and finding the right environment for studying, such as a quiet place in the library. *Understand* focuses on marking in your notes what you don't comprehend (so you can go back to it later). *Recall* is about being able to bring to mind key information when you've finished studying it. *Digest* centers on going back to the material you did not understand, trying again to comprehend it, and then internalizing the information to make it easier to recall. *Expand* focuses on applying the concepts you're learning, to make them more interesting and easier to remember. *Review* deals with going over all the material again (and again) until you are confident of your knowledge of it.

Study Stories

"One of the fundamental things I discovered—to my shock and amazement—is that I was never taught to study. I guess my teachers just assumed it would come naturally or something. And I guess it kind of did, as I always got good grades in school until I hit college. Luckily, I was taught a study system in one of my freshman classes, and that kind of opened my eyes to what I needed to be doing. I kind of do my own system now, partly because I have to study in different ways for different classes."

—Jill S.

PORPE, which stands for the words *predict, organize, rehearse, practice,* and *evaluate,* is a time-consuming study method in which you develop and answer essay questions to deepen your understanding of the material. *Predict* deals with trying to determine the most important concepts and formulating questions (starting with *compare, contrast, explain*) that will help you explain them. *Organize* revolves around summarizing the key information and then outlining answers to your predicted questions. *Rehearse* focuses on reciting aloud your key information and quizzing your memory of the material (usually over several days). *Practice* is answering your predicted questions from memory. *Evaluate* refers to assessing your answers to make certain they contain enough critical information and concrete examples.

> ### Study Stories
>
> "I realized, at some point, that my attitude was playing a pivotal role in my performance on tests. Because I did not do well on tests in my first semester, I later realized that my attitude going into tests was kind of negative—like self-defeatist. I would walk into tests thinking 'Sure hope I don't screw up another one.' I really think changing my attitude about tests played a big role in improving my grades, of course, but even just improving my studying techniques."
>
> —Steve B.

SQ3R, which stands for the words *survey, question, read, recite,* and *review,* is a popular system for both reading and studying. *Survey* revolves around gathering, skimming, and reviewing the information (notes, textbook) you need to learn. *Question* deals with raising issues as you are surveying (whether reviewing or reading), such as "What do I already know?" and "What did the professor emphasize in class?" *Read* involves rereading the material and looking for answers to the questions you raised previously. *Recite* deals with reviewing the material and putting the concepts into your own words (mentally or on paper), sometimes actually saying them out loud so that you also hear your words. *Review* is about the importance of going through the entire process again and again until you are confident you have comprehensive knowledge of the material.

The 4R's System includes *reducing, reciting, reflecting,* and *reviewing. Reducing* deals with organizing all the course information (lecture notes, handouts, readings) and condensing the information into small chunks of information. *Reciting* involves

> ### Study Stories
>
> "I usually have a lot of small study blocks. I always start with doing the study guide one day. Then I move on to the flash cards I made. Then I start on reading through my notes, and the next day I skim through the textbook. The day before the exam, I do all of the above."
>
> —Nicole Z.

speaking aloud about the reduced material without looking at it—talking through the ideas in your own words. *Reflecting* includes thinking about what you've learned, attempting to connect it with information and concepts you already know from previous work. *Reviewing* focuses on going through your notes several more times, concentrating on areas in which you still have some weakness, until you completely understand all the material you are studying.

Flash Cards

If you're like a lot of people, you probably have some experience with flash cards. Perhaps you used them to learn vocabulary words in middle school or to learn a foreign language in high school.

Flash cards are an especially useful study aid for general survey courses and other classes that include a lot of terminology or vocabulary. Just the process of creating the flash cards serves as a good tool to help you remember the material, but using them to test yourself on the concepts is really the strength of flash cards.

Study Stories

"When it comes time to study for the test, I usually start two to three days before the test. I go through my notes and make flash cards on what was important for those sections, paying special attention to what the teacher said would be on the test if there was a review session. Also, I go through the book and read the inset stories and add to my flash cards. Once the test is over, I keep the flash cards so that I have them for the next test or for the final."

—Laura B.

As you may recall, flash cards are pretty simple to make. On one side of an index card (or slip of paper of any type), you write the name of a term; on the other side, you write the definition (in your own words). Another alternative is to write a question on one side and then the answer to the question on the other side. You can also draw diagrams, pictures, and charts.

The idea when using flash cards to study is to use them to quiz yourself. Start by mixing them up (so you don't just memorize the information) and picking the card from the top. Look at the question or term, and then either write down or say out loud (because thinking the response is too passive): "The answer is …." Finally, turn the card over to see if you correctly and completely answered the question, explained the concept, or defined the term.

The great thing about flash cards is that you can take them anywhere. Whenever you have a break between classes or other activities, pull them out and test yourself.

One other alternative, especially if you get tired of quizzing yourself, is to use flash cards when you're studying with others.

Outlines

Outlines are a great study tool—but only once you have completed the readings, rewritten your notes, and organized your thinking, and are ready to consolidate your thinking.

Study Stories _____

"I make outlines and write out the key terms. I look at my notes sometime during the weeks before the test. I make sure that I have it all down the night before the test, and the next morning I get up for a two-hour cram study session to get it fresh in my head for the test that day. It works for me most of the time, but I am not the best test-taker in the world because I get too nervous! So I study as hard as I can—and that's the best I can do, as long as I've tried my best."

—Emily B.

A study-tool outline (compared to a chapter outline, for example) is your attempt to condense the large amounts of information you have from all your course sources into a logical system. In developing the outline, focus on broad subjects and key issues and concepts. Your goal in developing an outline is to put as much of the material on the front sides of just one or two pieces of paper. Once you've accomplished this task, you simply do all the rest of your studying from these sheets.

Study Suggestions _____

What is active learning, and why should you care about it? *Active learning* is a process in which you learn from others by (actively) engaging in higher-order thinking tasks such as questioning, analysis, synthesis, consolidation, and evaluation. Its value comes from the belief that, compared to passive learning techniques, you'll not only learn more material, but also retain the information much longer. Some studies show we retain 50 percent from discussions, 10 percent from reading, and 5 percent from class lectures. Active learning methods include discussion, debates, role-playing, and case study. Active learning is a key component of study groups.

Some professors and textbooks provide outlines of chapters, but use these only as a basis for developing your outline. In fact, never use someone else's outline: a large part of the benefit you get from this study tool is not the actual outline itself, but the process of whittling down the information to develop the outline.

Finally, remember that outlines do not need to be completely textual. You can also combine outlining with mind-mapping to create both a textual and visual outline. And, as always, do not spend so much time creating and perfecting the outline that you leave yourself too little time to actually study.

Study Groups

Studying with a group of your friends can be a fun and rewarding study method—as long as you pick group members wisely and follow a few rules. Study groups should not be your sole method of studying, but they can be a great supplement to your individual efforts. Unlike other types of studying, talking out issues in study groups is a form of active learning, the strongest kind of learning.

Studying with a group of people offers numerous benefits. You get to see the material from a different perspective, you stay motivated because the group needs you, and you commit more time to studying. In addition, group discussion helps you learn the material, and you get to share class notes and other materials, which means you can review material you might have missed and also pick up new study tips and habits.

Of course, anytime you have a group of people together, the biggest danger is getting off task, but you'll need to avoid some other problems as well. Try to avoid letting one member dominate the group, resist the urge to turn study sessions into gripe sessions, and make it a rule that group members must come prepared to participate and share.

How do you find people to join a study group? First, see if you can find peer students who share your academic goals and aspirations. Second, watch people in class and ask the students who appear attentive, take notes, and/or participate in class. Invite a few people to join your study group, with a goal of having about four or five people in the group. Finally, schedule an initial meeting of the group and see how everyone gets along. Ideal spaces for a study group are study rooms found in most libraries, as well as empty classrooms or conference rooms, but any place that has a table and chairs and some privacy should suit your needs. If all works out, proceed with establishing a few rules and scheduling regular meeting times.

> **Study Stories**
>
> "I prefer to study in small groups and practice problems where I can work out the methods verbally with others. I feel I learn better when I can teach other people information, and we can exchange notes taken in class because sometimes other students pick up on more important information than others."
>
> —Heather A.

Finally, here are a few suggestions for some study group guidelines to help you get the most from this study tool:

- Meet no more than two to three times a week.

- Keep sessions to no more than 60- to 90-minute periods.

- Establish responsibilities for each group member.

- Decide on study group management (permanent or rotating).

- Craft rules dealing with respect for each member.

- Share all contact information for group members.

Review Sessions

If you're lucky enough to have a professor who holds a review session—either regularly or before major tests—take advantage of this. Change your schedule, if you have to, but by all means attend.

Study Suggestions

As you've probably picked up by now (though it is certainly worth emphasizing), the more ways you can actively study, the better you can remember and retrieve the material you're studying. Talk out loud, walk around, create a short story or play, make up silly poems or mnemonic devices, and involve others in the discussion. Strategic learners use multiple study methods and tools to succeed.

By attending these review sessions, you'll have the chance to ask questions (and hear questions asked by other students), participate in discussion, develop strategies for studying the topics, possibly gain insight into how the professor may ask questions on the exam, and be seen as a student who takes the course seriously. And you never know when a question asked (and answered) in a review session will actually appear on the test.

Most faculty do not hold review sessions, citing a variety of reasons, including low turnout, inability of all students to attend, and not enough time for students with all their other obligations.

So what do you do if your professor does not hold review sessions? Hold your own! If you think a study group is a bit overwhelming, consider sort of a one-time study group by bringing together a group of students from class to hold your own review session. Who knows? If the professor hears about it, he or she might just stop in.

Study Suggestions

Here's a study rule you should always try to follow: do not try to learn anything new in the 24 hours before a test. As we've said in other parts of the book, cramming and trying to memorize course material the night before does you more harm than good—and certainly does *not* facilitate learning.

What should you bring to a review session? Bring your textbook, notebook, and questions about the material. (For math, accounting, or science review sessions, it might help to also bring a calculator.) Remember that review sessions are not a supplement to class—you still need to attend class.

> **Study Stories**
>
> "Studying for multiple tests and working on a few projects is something every college student experiences. How to get each task accomplished depends on planning ahead. As soon as I got my syllabus for each class, I would write the dates of important tests, projects, and papers so they wouldn't sneak up on me. I could start working on them in advance so that I wasn't left doing everything the night before."
>
> —Micaela H.

Developing Your Own Study Plan

Now that you've read about all of these study tools—and perhaps tried some of them—it's time to develop your own study plan. Remember to use multiple methods, with different techniques for different types of subjects and tests. Use this outline to help you get started on *your* system.

Action   **What It Entails**

_____   _____

                               _____

                               _____

                               _____

_____   _____

                               _____

                               _____

_____   _____

                               _____

                               _____

_____   _____
                    _____
                    _____
_____   _____
                    _____
                    _____

24-Hour Countdown

If you've followed any of the guidelines in this chapter, then by the time the day before the test arrives, you'll have been studying for several days, partaking in one or more active learning techniques designed to help you learn the material. If that's the case, what should your plan of attack be for the last 24 hours before the test?

Start the 24-hour clock with one last review of all your study materials, focusing on the most important details. If you have access to old or practice tests, do a simulated test. If you don't have access, consider making up your own test and then answering it.

Once you've completed this last bit of studying, reward yourself with something fun. Watch a movie, go bowling, have dinner with some friends. The best thing you can do for yourself the night before the test is let yourself (and your brain) relax a bit. No overdoing it—and certainly no drinking or other activities that will diminish your brain capabilities.

Go to bed at a decent hour and shoot for a solid night's sleep. Sleep provides another perfect opportunity for the brain to recharge.

In the morning, eat a light breakfast, especially if the test is in the morning. Food does fuel the brain. Don't overdo the caffeine because too much of it just makes you overanxious and can tax the brain. If your test is in the afternoon, make sure you have a light lunch. If you feel the need and have an hour break before the test, review the basics—but don't test yourself or go too deeply into the material; save that for the test.

What You've Learned

Ready for a quick check to see what you've learned from this chapter? I now understand …

◆ The best study technique is one that I start at least a week before the actual test.

◆ I need to find—or develop—a study tool that best works for me.

◆ I should consider multiple study methods to increase my learning and knowledge of the material.

◆ Active learning techniques—in which I am physically or mentally doing things—are much better than passive ones.

◆ I should consider using my classmates and my professor as key partners in my study method.

The Least You Need to Know

◆ Using one or more study tools is an effective way to learn and apply material—and not just memorize it.

◆ The best study techniques for me should focus on active techniques that best fit my learning style.

◆ Effective studying starts long before a test.

◆ Taking a longer-term view of studying will help in studying smarter, not harder.

Chapter 9

Testing Techniques

In This Chapter

- ◆ Review the importance of good test preparation
- ◆ Examine all the major types of college tests
- ◆ Find insights and tips for succeeding on tests

This chapter is all about succeeding on any and all types of tests. Assuming you have been applying all the advice from previous chapters to your arsenal of study skills, this chapter provides tips, tools, and strategies for helping you achieve success with all the major types of tests you'll face in college.

We'll start by reviewing some basic test-preparation strategies. We'll discuss the importance of practice tests and then delve into the details of objective exams (multiple-choice and true/false questions), short-answer exams, essay exams, and open-book and take-home exams.

By the time you're done with this chapter, you'll be an expert on taking any type of exam!

Test-Prep Basics

There's no substitute for test preparation—no secret tricks. And you know by now that we do not support cramming for an exam except under the most dire of circumstances—and our top students agree.

The best students plan well in advance of a test. Some students prepare from the first day of class, devising a study schedule that is basically a test-preparation schedule: through daily review and study, they are truly learning the course material. Most other students generally start test preparation anywhere from a week to a few days before the scheduled exam.

Test preparation, of course, really began much earlier in the book, when we discussed the importance of reading and learning material from your textbook, taking and rewriting strong class notes, and reviewing and developing the best study tools that work for you.

But now the test looms a week ahead, so let's look at what you should be doing to prepare for it. The first thing you need to do is set a goal for what you hope to achieve on the test. To motivate themselves, some students set a goal of an A—or even a perfect score. Don't make your goal so unrealistic that it demotivates you, but do strive for a goal that is an extra stretch for you so that you will be motivated to study—to keep a positive attitude and help you succeed.

The next step is to block out some time in the days leading up to the test—and always give yourself more time for studying so that you can take breaks and also deal with any unexpected things that might interfere with your study efforts (such as fire alarms going off or friends dropping by to cheer you up). Remember, too, in developing your schedule that you want to finish studying the day *before* the exam.

The final step is to organize all your study materials—chapter outlines/summaries, homework assignments, and class notes. Use these materials to develop the study tool(s) you learned about in Chapter 8, and start studying! We recommend testing yourself on the material, which we'll get to in the next section.

Having the Right Mental Attitude

Test preparation is all about having the right mental attitude so that you can concentrate and learn the material. Still, you should be prepared for common occurrences that can affect your ability to maintain that positive attitude:

◆ Too much pressure from home to succeed. Consider asking your family to not talk about a critical exam in the time leading up to it.

◆ Problems with your roommate. If your roommate is not cooperating, find somewhere else on campus, such as the library, to study.

◆ Emotional issues with a friend or significant other. Try to settle these situations as quickly as possible. Otherwise, emotional difficulties will linger in your brain and block out all else.

◆ Work-related concerns, such as too many hours of work or troubles with a boss or co-worker. Don't let work interfere with your academic success, if at all possible.

Study Stories

"The best word to describe my test preparation is *thorough*. I don't take any shortcuts because they usually don't work. I read the material and outline it so that I can read over my notes a couple times before the exam … I have to put in the time, but it always pays off. I make a realistic plan before I start studying for a test. I can estimate how long it takes me to complete a chapter, and then I plan accordingly."

—Jessica H.

Tips in Situations in Which You Must Cram

If there is no way around it and you must cram (which you should *never* have to do—and something top students never do), here are some quick tips for doing so:

◆ Review all the material and pick the five or six most important concepts, main ideas, or key formulas.

◆ Create a sheet for each of your five or six items, with bullet points for important supporting elements. Don't get bogged down in too many details (because you just won't remember them).

◆ If you haven't read the text, now is not the time to start; instead, read the chapter summaries and key terms—and add points, where appropriate, on your sheets of paper.

◆ When your sheets are done, alternate studying (and possibly rewriting) each sheet with a short study break between each one. During each break, stretch, relax, eat, or exercise.

◆ If possible, avoid too much caffeine and sugar during your cramming, and get some sleep before the exam to give your brain a chance to recharge.

◆ Have a back-up alarm to get you up, since you'll be working on limited sleep.

◆ Wake up and review your sheets one more time before you take the exam.

◆ Eat something healthful and nutritious before taking the exam.

If you feel your stress building to levels that begin blocking your ability to study, jump to Chapter 14 for some great tips for dealing with and managing stress.

Your goal with all this test preparation is to wake up on the test day and feel confident and prepared. Most students have some degree of test anxiety, but if you've prepared well for the test, that anxiety should be minimal. Some anxiety can be good because it increases your adrenaline and raises your energy level.

Study Suggestions

If you have extreme test anxiety—regardless of how much studying you do—and find yourself just completely freezing up during exams, you should immediately seek help from your school's counseling center or academic support center. There's no shame in admitting that you are having difficulty coping with the stress—and it's much better to seek assistance and get good grades than suffer (both personally and academically) without it.

Don't forget to make a list of any equipment you need for the test, such as pens, pencils, calculators, and equations—and then make sure you actually take it all with you the day of the test! Consider dressing comfortably for the exam, possibly wearing layers to deal with temperature variations.

Try to get to class a few minutes early so that you can get settled into your seat and do a few relaxation techniques (such as taking a few deep breaths). If some students around you are panicking and talking about the test—something we always hated when we were students—step out of the room and simply just walk around a bit to help clear your mind. Don't forget to turn off your cell phone!

Study Suggestions

Don't let a learning disability stop you from achieving academic success. All colleges offer special assistance to students with learning disabilities, so if you have one—or think you do—go immediately to your school's academic support center and determine what you need to do to get the assistance you need.

Once the class begins and you receive the test, the single most important thing you need to do is *carefully* listen to the instructor's verbal directions *and* thoroughly read the test instructions. Some tests have multiple parts, with some optional and mandatory questions—and you want to make sure you completely understand what you need to accomplish before you jump into answering the questions. If you don't understand any part of the questions, ask the professor or test proctor.

Finally, before you begin responding to the questions, most experts advise two other strategies. First, consider writing down important formulas, processes, and keywords in a margin so you don't have to worry about forgetting them when you get to the questions. (This process is what some people refer to as "doing a brain dump.") Second, make a quick and strategic plan for the order in which you'll answer the questions, typically starting with those questions with the highest point value. (Note that some experts recommend that students who are feeling overly anxious tackle the easy questions first, to reduce anxiety and build confidence.)

Study Stories

"I have a couple of rituals I go through before big exams. I don't know if they really help or not, but ever since I started doing these things, I have done really well on my exams. I have a special set of songs on my iPod that I listen to the night before—in between doing some last-minute studying. They're just silly songs really, but they pump me up and get my blood going. Then in the morning, before I head to breakfast, I watch a clip from one of my favorite movies—it's just totally inspiring and sends me off with a great attitude and a smile. I also bring my iPod with me in case I get to class too early and people are talking about the test. Rather than getting caught up in all that, I just tune it out ... literally."

—Jill S.

As you're taking the test, watch your time carefully. Don't spend too long lingering over questions with small point values, only to have too little time to complete answers to questions with high point values.

Study Suggestions

What do you do if you get to a question—especially one with a high point value—and you're completely stuck? You either don't quite get the question or you have a mental block. First, relax your mind for a second or two. Then try rewriting the question. If that doesn't help, and your professor allows it, go up and ask her to help clarify it for you. If you still don't get it, try to move on to the rest of the test; come back to it at the end and see if you can tackle it then.

To relax yourself during the exam, consider changing positions, doing a few breathing techniques, or simply stretching from your seat. Don't let people who complete the test extremely quickly bother you; there's no reward in finishing first, but there is a reward for finishing completely and to the best of your ability.

If you have the time, before submitting your exam, review it to make certain you answered all the questions and did not accidentally mismark the answer sheet or make any other errors. If you guessed on some of the questions, most experts say the first response is usually the best, so avoid doing too much second-guessing at this point and turn in your exam. (If you do have to guess at any responses, guess intelligently by first eliminating any obvious wrong answers.)

Study Suggestions _____

This tip might sound obvious, but we've found that a lot of students don't do it, so we're including it here for you. If a test has bonus questions on it, just do them! Bonus responses can't hurt you—and just a few bonus points can boost your grade.

Practice Tests

You may know the old saying "Practice makes perfect," and that certainly applies to test preparation, too. Our brains are wired in such a way that the more times we do something, the better information is retained. More than a hundred years ago, philosopher and psychologist William James wrote: "My experience is what I agree to attend to. Only those items which I notice shape my mind—without selective interest, experience is an utter chaos."

What does it all mean for you in your quest for greater academic achievement? It means that your last step before you actually take the real test is to work on perfecting your knowledge and skills with one or more practice exams.

As we discussed in Chapter 3, some professors actually put old exams on reserve in the campus library—or even online on the department website. If your professor doesn't, you should consider asking if he or she is willing to do so.

Study Suggestions _____

Almost regardless of the subject, there are only so many ways to ask the same question. Thus, the more previous exams or practice tests you review, the more likely you will find questions on the actual exam that are extremely close to those you've already answered during your practice. This should make it much easier for you to answer, and to answer well.

Another option for finding practice exams is going to the source—to the publisher of your course textbook. Many general subject courses have study guides, which include practice quizzes and tests. A more recent development is a dedicated website for the textbook, which includes chapter outlines, key terms, quizzes, tests, and more. And because textbook publishers also provide test banks to professors, you are likely to see very similarly worded questions on the actual exam.

> **Study Stories**
>
> "I've never been a good test-taker—and that affected my attitude and also my performance and grades. Besides slowly changing my attitude, the other thing I did—kind of by accident one semester when a professor told me to review his old exams—was that I now actively seek out old exams for every class I take. I'm not trying to cheat or anything, though sometimes I feel a little guilty when a question on the exam is exactly the same as on the practice exam. I just know that taking a practice exam kind of eases my mind and helps me keep a positive attitude. And it has definitely raised my grades!"
>
> —Steve B.

A final option in your quest for practice exams is to consider developing one yourself. If you've been given a study guide or been told what to expect on the exam, you should be able to develop your own test. Even better, if you're part of a study group (see Chapter 8) or are simply studying with a friend, you can each compose a practice exam and then share it with each other. Then you can answer one or more of other people's practice exams.

The bottom line here is that you should make an extraordinary effort to find or develop practice exams, especially for the first test of any course, in which you are totally unfamiliar with how the professor tests on the course material.

Objective Exams

Objective exams are tests in which there is only one correct answer to the questions. Examples of objective exams include multiple-choice, true/false, fill-in-the-blank, and matching questions.

Objective exams test your ability to recognize the correct answer. Objective exams are extremely popular for testing your ability to define terminology, so if you're in a course with a lot of new (to you) vocabulary, you can certainly expect to see some objective questions on the exams.

Pacing is important with objective questions, as you'll typically have about a minute per question.

Study Suggestions

What do you do if you hit a question for which you have no idea of the answer? First, of course, try to deduce the answer by thoroughly examining the question. If you still don't know the answer, take a guess—and stick to it. Experts generally state that your first hunch is the correct one, so avoid second-guessing yourself when you don't know the answer. Don't ever leave a multiple-choice or true/false question blank.

Multiple-Choice Questions

Multiple-choice questions come in several different forms, from straight definitions to analogies to problem solving. Among a choice of responses, there's one correct (best, true) answer, and it's your job to find it.

Your initial strategy is to read the question carefully—perhaps several times, if necessary, to understand it (especially looking for modifiers such as *always, only, most, all, never, completely, best, worst, smallest, largest*). Then before you look at the choices provided, answer the question in your own words.

Next, unless you immediately spot the response that matches your answer, your task is to first eliminate the obviously false and implausible responses, ideally narrowing your choice to two final possibilities. Typically, general statements are more likely to be correct than specific ones. Don't choose responses that include words that you don't know or have never seen.

Finally, be especially wary of multiple-response questions—"all of the above," "none of the above," or some combination of choices. You'll need to treat each of these responses as true/false situations—and answer accordingly.

Study Suggestions

If you have the time, a good way of to read objective exam questions is to underline key terms and clue words in the question. (Example: According to your readings and our classroom discussions, the <u>basic premise</u> of <u>marketing</u> is:) By eliminating other words from the question, you should more clearly understand the question—and answer it correctly.

True/False Questions

True/false questions can be the most annoying type of questions for students because so many of these questions typically have some degree of ambiguity to them. The premise of a true/false question is simple: you are presented with a statement that you must judge to be true or false.

Generally, a statement has to be completely true for you to select *true* as your response, whereas if any part of the statement is false, then your response should be *false*. Be careful of reading too much into the question—answer it on its face value. (In fact, some experts say true/false questions are actually harder for good students, who tend to linger over each question and read much too much into it.)

Researchers have also found a few patterns with true/false questions that may assist you. Statements that contain the words *all, only, always,* and *solely* are typically false. Statements containing the words *likely, frequently, generally,* and *usually* are typically true. Also, exaggerated or complex statements are generally false. Finally, if you're totally unsure of whether a statement is true or false, mark it as true.

Study Suggestions

When you're taking a math or science exam, it's a good idea to double-check your calculations before choosing a response.

Fill-in-the-Blank/Sentence-Completion Questions

Fill-in-the-blank questions require a much deeper knowledge of the subject and are written in such a way that one or more words are missing. You must write in the correct response.

In some cases, you may have a list of words to choose from for these types of questions, but more often than not, you'll need to supply the correct term(s).

Keep in mind some basic rules for answering these types of questions. Unless otherwise stated, it's typically one word per blank. Several blank lines separated by commas indicate a series of responses. Several blank lines without commas point toward a response in the form of a phrase.

For these types of exam questions, you're pretty much out of luck if you can't remember the name/date/equation of the response. As a way to jog your memory, reread the question several times because the response may unexpectedly jump into your mind. As a last-ditch effort to get partial credit, you can try to write some sort of explanation or definition to show you understand the question but just can't remember the exact answer.

> **Study Suggestions**
>
> Be very careful of negatives, which can be expressed as words (*none, no, not*) or prefixes (*il-, un-, im-*). When you read questions quickly, you can easily miss negatives. Some professors (intentionally or not) also include double negatives in their questions, such as: "It's impossible to assume that causes of World War I were not due to rising political strife in Europe."

Matching Questions

With matching questions, you'll find two columns of material; your goal is to match the items in the first column with the items in the second column. In some cases, there will be an exactly equal number to choose from, while in other situations there may be extra—false—responses to choose from. Matching questions are like multiple, multiple-choice questions—which raises the complexity and can lead to a domino effect of incorrect responses/matches.

Your best strategy with matching questions is to read all of the choices, match the items that you are certain of, cross off the choices that you have used, and then proceed with the remaining items.

Finally, analyze the remaining choices to determine whether any parts of them will allow you to deduce possible matching choices.

Short-Answer Exams

Short-answer questions are open-ended questions that require students to create some sort of answer. Short-answer items typically require responses from a few sentences to several paragraphs. They may also involve writing out formulas or completing math calculations. Be sure you have an idea of the amount of information the professor is seeking.

Your strategy with short-answer questions is to carefully read and reread the question and identify the key pieces of information you need to provide in your response. Typically, short-answer questions can be written in bullet or list format, with the emphasis on information rather than on quality writing.

Study Stories

"I used to dread taking essay tests, for a couple of reasons. Partly, I just never liked having to know the material so deeply as you do for essay questions—I mean, part of it was the courses themselves. But the other part was just not being confident in my writing, so I never wanted to have to rely on it for a good grade. Looking back, I kind of wish I had taken more writing classes because I have certainly come to use it quite a bit as a junior and senior."

—Jill S.

Essay Exams

Professors are seeking a comprehensive analysis when they use essay questions, not simply a brain dump on the subject at hand. Seek out key words that will help you answer the question, such as *summarize, defend, trace, solve, explain, list, debate, clarify, describe, compare,* and *contrast.* You should underline these key words that relate to how the professor wants you to answer the question. Following are some of these key words and what your task is when answering the essay question.

- **Compare:** Examine similarities and differences, and come to a conclusion.

- **Describe:** Provide a detailed account, including significant characteristics and traits.

- **Discuss:** Present arguments, analyze advantages and disadvantages, and present pros and cons.

- **Explain:** State reasons or justifications for something, or how and why something occurred.

- **Illustrate:** Provide examples to demonstrate or prove the subject of the question, sometimes with a visual element, such as a graph or diagram.

- **Review:** Report on the important ideas and major points, and briefly comment on them.

Study Suggestions

An easy-to-remember process for answering essay questions is the ROW method:

Read the question several times to make certain you thoroughly understand what is being asked of you. Some essay questions have multiple parts.

Outline the main points you want to cover in your answer in the margins, on the back of the test, or on a piece of scrap paper.

Write your essay, confidently answering the question(s) with the outline you developed. Remember to include a broad opening paragraph and a concluding closing paragraph.

As best you can—especially in such a stressful situation—write your essay answers following basic principles of writing, including using topic sentences, writing in paragraph form with full sentences, employing strong transitions, and providing details and examples to support your arguments. It's best to start your essay response by first paraphrasing the question and providing a concise answer that you will then explain and support in the following paragraphs.

If the teacher allows it, certainly consider using bullets or a numbered list to more clearly show your key points. Avoid excessive wordiness and rambling because these actions make it appear that you do not know the answer.

Finally, if you have the time, reread your answers and proofread and fix any errors you find. You'll find many more writing tips and suggestions in Part 4, starting with Chapter 11.

Open-Book and Take-Home Exams

Students often get very excited about the possibility of an open-book or take-home exam, yet, in some ways, these exam methods are much harder than students ever expect. Because these exams appear to require less study time, students are often caught off-guard in their preparations.

Unlike other types of tests that measure your level of recall or memorization, these types of tests measure your level of understanding.

In an open-book exam, students are allowed to refer to the textbook, notes, and/or a one-page study sheet or index card. Take-home exams, in which you are given the questions ahead of the test due date, should be treated more like papers than exams.

The best way to prepare for these types of exams—besides the obvious techniques we've been discussing this entire book—is to carefully organize all your course materials so that you can find the information you need quickly and efficiently. For example, use sticky pads to label sections of your textbook and notes so you can easily locate the information you seek. Create summary sheets for all the key concepts and theories, and include where you can find more details in your notes and actual pages numbers from your textbook(s).

Study Stressors

The worst thing you can do is to take an open-book or take-home exam too lightly. You must do a fair amount of preparation. If you don't properly prepare for it, you'll find yourself scrambling and you'll be in a somewhat panicked state during the test.

Finally, as with all the other exam types we've mentioned in this chapter, take the time to carefully read the questions so that you fully understand the best way to respond.

What You've Learned

Ready for a quick check to see what you've learned from this chapter? I now understand ...

- How to prepare for my tests.
- The value of using practice exams to help me prepare.
- Strategies I should follow when taking multiple-choice, true/false, and other objective exams.
- Tactics for dealing with short-answer exams.
- Ways to approach essay exams.
- How to tackle open-book and take-home exams.

The Least You Need to Know

- The best way to prepare for any type of exam is through a thorough review of all your material—readings, notes, and homework assignments.
- Taking practice exams—whether from the textbook, a collection of old tests, or those you compose yourself—is a good way to prepare for the real thing.
- Regardless of the testing technique, it's always extremely important to read the instructions for taking the exam.
- Remember to carefully examine how the professor has worded test questions, looking for keywords that should help you answer the questions correctly.

Chapter 10

Subjects That Require Special Study Techniques

In This Chapter

- ◆ Learn study techniques for raising math scores
- ◆ Discover how to achieve success in science courses
- ◆ Acquire skills that will help with English classes
- ◆ Find study tips for improving foreign language grades

Certain subjects require a bit more specialized attention. You may already be an achiever in one or more of these subject areas, but for most of us, these subjects require a few more skills and techniques to conquer.

These courses are certainly not tougher than other courses you'll face in your college career, but they stand out as ones that some students stumble in. Perhaps that's because they all are typically taken in the first two years of college—and because just about all college students have to take them.

Thus, this chapter focuses on specific study techniques for the four subjects that tend to give trouble to the vast majority of college students: math, science, English, and foreign language.

Math

Of all the subjects that cause fear in students, math is probably at the top of the list. Some students swear that their brains are just not programmed for math, which then sets in motion a vicious cycle of fear and anxiety.

Math is also different because it's applied—learned from completing practice problems. This, in turn, helps you learn formulas and techniques for solving other math problems. And college math is different from high school math because the pace tends to be much faster, most work is completed outside of class, and professors rarely correct your homework.

Besides attending every class, the best students try to complete the homework assignments later that same day after class—while the new formulas and such are fresh in their minds. Before beginning your problem set, review your notes and the formulas you learned, then apply them to the homework problems. Consider doing more problems than the professor assigned.

> **Study Stories**
>
> "Math is all about practice. Actually doing problems is the only way you learn math. Most professors use questions from the homework, but with different numbers for the test. It's about understanding the process."
>
> —Stephanie G.

> **Study Suggestions**
>
> Because math is a cumulative subject—today's lesson builds for tomorrow's—if you ever have to miss a class, it's imperative that you meet with your professor during office hours and make certain that you understand the material you missed. If you don't, you may be lost or struggling for weeks—or for the rest of the term.

As you go about reading the math textbook, here are some suggestions:

◆ Schedule a big block of time so you don't have to rush.

◆ Find a quiet place because math especially requires good concentration.

◆ Take the time to flip through the pages of the chapter before you actually start reading it.

◆ Carefully read—and make certain you understand—each term, formula, and symbol before moving on to the next section of the chapter.

◆ Record key formulas, properties, and the like in your notes; consider putting them on flash cards, too.

◆ Never skip over diagrams, graphs, charts, or any other illustrative materials.

◆ Work out all problems as you go through the book. Be sure you understand the processes the text authors use to solve the problems.

About a week before a math test, try to increase your problem-solving time, perhaps even working with a few other students from class. Rework old homework problems. Complete similar math problems. Consider asking the professor for some examples of old tests so you can further perfect your problem-solving abilities. Finally, make sure you get a good night's sleep before the test.

Study Stories _____

"With math classes, always do the assigned problems—but don't stop there. Also try to do the problems that weren't assigned. You might be happily surprised when the test comes around—my professor typically had a problem or two right from the book, but always ones he had not assigned as homework."

—Steve B.

Once you're at the test, here are a few key test-taking strategies:

- Take the time to examine the entire test so that you get a sense of the number and type of problems.

- Complete the exam in whatever order works best for you, typically starting with the problems you are most confident about solving.

- Always do all your work on the test itself so that if a simple math error throws off your answer, the professor can assign you partial credit based on your knowledge shown in your work.

- With more complex math problems, try to break down the problem into its various subparts—and complete as many of those parts as you can.

- Watch the clock. Math problems can be so engaging that you accidentally spend more time than you should, so monitor your progress carefully.

> **Study Stories**
>
> "With math, you just have to do all the practice problems; it's just like playing an instrument—you have to practice in order for the music to flow."
>
> —Jessy H.

In terms of word problems, which often give math test-takers extra aggravation as they try to translate the story into a mathematical expression, here is one formula for helping solve the puzzle—the UPS Method:

- **Understand**—In this step, you need to determine which pieces of information are important and what exactly the problem is asking you to find. Cross out any irrelevant information.

- **Plan**—This step is all about determining how you will solve the problem. You may need to draw or otherwise visualize the problem to help you determine the best method for solving.

- **Solve**—You complete the mathematical calculations in this step to arrive at the solution. Check your solution for logic (could this number really be the answer?) and calculation errors.

As you progress through the course, remember to keep completing all homework assignments and quizzes—every point counts! Some experts also suggest practicing positive self-talk—for example, "I believe I can succeed in math class"—as a way to build a positive attitude and help overcome math anxiety.

If you're struggling with math—or are afraid you will—here are four ways you can get the help you need:

♦ Visit your math professor during office hours and attend any extra workshops or help sessions she or he offers.

♦ Use the resources of your school's math tutoring lab. If your school does not offer one, consider hiring an upper-division math student to personally tutor you.

♦ Form a math study group with some of your classmates.

♦ Find other math resources, such as the math websites we list in the appendix.

Finally, if you have to take more than one math course in college, try to take them consecutively—partly to get them over with, but mainly because math builds on itself.

Study Stories _____

"I was absolutely terrified of math. In fact, the first time I took it, the professor gave a test on the first day. I was so freaked out, I never went back to the class and eventually dropped it. Only later did I learn that the professor does a pretest on the first day to get a feel for everyone's skills level so he can tailor some of the early lessons. When I took it the second time, I was a little more confident because I knew more of what to expect—plus, I got to know the professor and he often gave me extra homework problems."

—Jill S.

Sciences

As with the study of math, many students find studying the sciences to be somewhat of a challenge. Unlike in some other disciplines, students need to know the material and also how to apply it and manipulate it. Many science courses also include a lab class in addition to the lecture, in which you apply some of the lessons from class to actual experiments and write reports explaining your findings.

You'll typically have at least one lab partner, but you should also continue collaboration outside of lab to include the entire course. With so much information at the college level, study groups help you learn all the material at a more acceptable pace.

Doing well in science classes requires a deeper understanding than you'll get from simply reading the textbook and attending class. You'll need to understand the interrelationships of multiple variables, theories, principles, and rules. Typically, you'll also be expected to know (and often recreate on exams) diagrams, charts, and graphs depicting these interrelationships, as well as specific terminology. Of all the courses in college, many high-achieving students stress the importance of using multiple study techniques (utilizing all your learning styles) and setting aside more time for studying than for other classes.

Study Suggestions

If you do not plan to be a science major, seek out science classes that are designed for nonscience majors. These classes will still be rigorous, but not nearly at the level for majors.

Study Stories

"If you do the practice problems, you will understand the material so much better because science is not just memorization, like history; you need to be able to apply what you have learned in a practical situation."

—Laura B.

A key component of your science grade involves your lab work—especially your lab report. While some professors may give you an outline of what they specifically seek, here is one for the many professors who do not:

- **Abstract**—A short description/overview of the entire lab report, including the procedures, outcomes, and conclusions. Typically, this is anywhere from 100 to 250 words.

- **Introduction**—Background information and the key issue or problem related to the experiment. Some reports include a statement of the specific hypothesis you tested.

- **Procedures**—The materials and methods you used, including the experimental design, apparatus, and methods of gathering and analyzing data.

- **Results**—The data from your experiment, without any interpretation or conclusions. Often this includes tables, graphs, and diagrams to present the data in a more comprehensible form.

- **Discussion/ conclusion**—The significance of the results you presented in the previous section. Here you show how the results support your hypothesis or explain why they differ from what you expected. You also include any patterns and relationships that emerged from the research.

- **Appendixes**—More detailed information or calculations, including additional tables and figures, that supplement the report.

 Study Stressors

Reading and comprehending a science textbook can be challenging. The key is not to become overwhelmed by the scientific jargon and complex diagrams and charts—you'll lose focus. Be prepared to read the text multiple times—and at least once before you attend class lecture on the topic.

Which science is right for you? Here's a basic overview of the major sciences:

◆ **Astronomy**—The study of the planets, stars, galaxies, and universe as a whole, including their origins and how they evolved over time.

◆ **Biology**—The study of living organisms: how they live, interact with other living things, and evolve.

◆ **Botany**—The study of plants: how they function, what they look like, how they are related to each other, where they grow, and how they evolve.

◆ **Chemistry**—The study of how the physical world operates, examining the atomic and molecular structure of matter.

◆ **Environmental science**—The study of interactions among the physical, chemical, and biological components of the environment.

◆ **Geography**—The study of the relationships among Earth's landscapes, people, places, and environment.

◆ **Geology**—The study of Earth, its history, and how Earth's materials, structures, processes, and organisms have changed over time.

◆ **Physics**—The study of the fundamental laws of nature governing the inner workings of everything. The interaction of matter and energy.

◆ **Zoology**—The study of animals and their ecosystems, including animal behavior, evolution, genetics, and ecology.

English

Unless you test out of it, most first-year college students can expect to take two required English classes—some combination of college writing, composition, and analytical reading and writing. First-year English classes are designed to develop your writing skills and introduce literacy concepts that help you successfully navigate a broad array of writing challenges; they are intended, in short, to help you improve your writing.

Study Stories

"I thought I was a pretty good writer when I was in high school, but my freshman composition class was an eye-opening experience for me. At first, I hated it because I felt the professor devalued my writing. But as the semester went on and I began to use the writing handbook and writing center, I learned that my writing skills were pretty mediocre. By changing my attitude, I was able to become a much better writer—and it has served me extremely well in later essay exams, papers, and projects."
—Jill S.

If you've never really enjoyed reading and writing, college is now the time to try to embrace them. The skills you'll develop and sharpen in your college English courses will serve you admirably—not only through college, but in your career as well. Good writing (as we discuss more in Part 4) is an essential tool for academic success—and it all begins in these first-year English classes.

Study Stories

"Leave yourself plenty of time to write essays and papers. They take time to get all the information out of your head and onto the page, so don't leave them until the last second."
—Laura B.

There are several keys to success in first-year English classes. Following these tips should put you in good shape for academic success:

♦ Embrace your writing handbook. The writing handbook your college uses should become your key reference for all things related to planning, writing, revising, editing, and polishing your English assignments.

♦ Gain an appreciation for literature. Because at least one of your English classes will involve reading a collection of essays or other literary works, embrace the readings as a chance to become more worldly and sophisticated.

◆ Advance your writing beyond the five-paragraph format. Many high-school students learn to write using this simple formula, but college writing is much more complex. The sooner you leave that format—or any other rigid rules of writing—behind, the better your writing will become.

◆ Find the writing center. One of your best resources on campus (besides your professor) is the writing center/writing lab, where trained tutors provide individual assistance on all types of writing assignments.

◆ Don't take shortcuts. These first-year English classes will give you the foundation of skills necessary to become a better writer, so avoid taking shortcuts, such as borrowing or plagiarizing (see Chapter 11) other people's work or paying someone else to write or draft your papers.

◆ Use online resources. For most students in first-year English classes, the professor, the texts, and the writing center will be your main tools for success. However, numerous online resources (especially online writing centers) can also help you. We've listed some of these in the appendix.

◆ Discover ways to unblock yourself. Many writers of all ages talk about writing anxiety and writer's block—the inability to put words to paper because of a pessimistic feeling about writing. The best way to overcome this situation is to take a fresh and positive view of the assignment and your writing abilities.

Finally, in at least one of your first-year English classes, you'll be writing critical essays about novels, essays, stories, poems, music, or works of art. Here's a short overview of the key ingredients of a critical essay:

◆ **Introduction**—Describes the work you are analyzing. Includes your thesis/theme (such as the work's strengths and weaknesses, method of writing, or meanings of key characters).

◆ **Description/summary**—Reviews the major points and background of the work to refresh the reader's memory of it. This section contains no analysis—simply a summary.

- ◆ **Interpretation/analysis/criticism**—Focuses on evaluating and analyzing the work as it relates to your thesis. Use specific examples from the work to support your point of view.

- ◆ **Conclusion**—Summarizes the main points of your analysis, restating both your thesis and the key points you made to support it.

Study Suggestions

Learn to embrace your English classes. These courses will help build your knowledge, appreciation, and quality of writing. Good writing will help you in just about every other course in college. As a business professor explained to a student who received a letter-grade reduction because of poor writing and complained that it was not an English course, "Every course in college is an English course."

Foreign Languages

Many colleges and universities require students to attain at least some level of competency with one or more foreign languages.

Study Suggestions

If you're lucky enough to have a gift for languages, strive to become multilingual. Not only will learning other languages help you with English, but having this skill on your resumé will make you much more marketable as a job seeker. In most other countries outside the United States, vast numbers of the population are either bilingual or multilingual.

Whether or not you have been exposed to a foreign language, learning a language other than your native tongue is not an easy task for most students. But if you stick with it—study the other language in depth, read and write in it, and have conversations in it—you'll actually understand more about English at the same time.

Study Stories _____

"Practice communication with friends! Straight memorization never works with foreign languages because it's all in the applications of the words and grammar. Study with friends, have dialogues in that language, and figure out ways together to remember certain words."
—Jessica W.

Whether you have to learn another language or simply want to do it to better yourself, here are some tips to make the learning process easier:

◆ Immerse yourself in the language. Make studying or using the foreign language a part of every single day. The more time you invest in the language, the better you'll learn it.

◆ Attend every class. This advice can certainly apply to all your courses, but learning a language is cumulative, so it's especially important.

◆ Buy a good foreign-language dictionary and expand your knowledge of vocabulary beyond what you're learning in the classroom.

◆ Download materials written or recorded in the foreign language—or watch a foreign-language cable show—and practice your translation skills.

◆ Use the foreign language lab—a library of sorts dedicated to helping students learn a foreign language—to sharpen your skills.

◆ Practice speaking the foreign language with classmates.

Study Stories _____

"Practice. It is hard to succeed in a foreign language class if you are just showing up and doing the work. But if you're in your room and look at objects and try to say them in the foreign language you are learning, it actually helps."
—Sarah P.

Which foreign language(s) should you study? It partly depends on your personal interests and your career interests—and, of course, many students simply continue with the foreign language they learned in high school. Here's a list of the modern languages offered at many larger universities:

- Spanish
- French
- Italian
- German

Study Suggestions

We have to put in a plug for studying Latin, at least as a supplemental language. We're both Latin scholars and can attest to its value as a great foundation for all the Romance languages (Spanish, Portuguese, French, Italian, Romanian), as well as for building your English vocabulary.

Less common, but growing in number, are these languages:

- Chinese
- Arabic
- Japanese

Study Stories

"For anyone who's serious about learning another language, I highly recommend staying in another country and practicing your conversation skills. Being able to conjugate verbs on paper means nothing if you cannot speak or use them properly in sentences, or be able to listen to someone."

—Morgan S.

What You've Learned

Ready for a quick check to see what you've learned from this chapter? I now understand ...

◆ The best methods for studying math.

◆ Success strategies for doing well in a science class.

◆ Tactics for excelling in first-year English classes.

◆ The value and importance of learning—as well as how to learn—a foreign language.

The Least You Need to Know

◆ The best way to get better at math is to keep working out as many math problems as you can—including completing all the math homework problems.

◆ Studying for a science course takes more of a time commitment than other classes, especially when a lab is involved.

◆ First-year English classes give students a writing foundation that will be useful in most other college courses.

◆ Studying a foreign language is a valuable tool for personal and career development—but because of its cumulative effect, it takes a great deal of time and dedication to learn.

Part 4

Succeeding with Writing

Learning to write well is a study skill you'll want to master. It's also a skill that will serve you well after college: about two thirds of salaried workers have jobs that require writing, and professionals spend almost a third of their days writing.

The first two chapters of this part take you through the steps in writing a major college paper, from research to proofreading and revising. These chapters also focus on pitfalls to avoid in research and writing. The third chapter describes how to succeed with the most common types of writing assignments.

Chapter 11

Research Methods

In This Chapter

- ◆ Discover techniques to develop a research topic
- ◆ Learn to conduct a productive keyword search
- ◆ Find out about the best research resources
- ◆ Get the lowdown on organizing and integrating research

Research is not only the backbone of most of the writing assignments you will complete in college; it also is a significant skill that you will sharpen and fine-tune as a college student. You may have learned and developed some research skills in high school, but in college, you are expected to become much more sophisticated and scholarly in your use of research. This chapter helps you do that and guides you in developing topics for research and writing.

Conducting research is a critical element in preparing a writing assignment because the direction of your research shapes the direction of your paper. It usually doesn't work well to conduct research on the fly once you've started writing; you'll likely be much more successful if you gather all your research first (which means starting early!), organize your research, and then determine how to integrate your research into your paper as you begin writing.

Let's begin with definitions of the major sources of research you will consider as you prepare a written assignment:

Primary sources are published original writings, reflections, and reports that you can find in books, periodicals, monographs, conference proceedings, patents, and theses and dissertations.

Secondary sources are published writings and reports that analyze, critique, or report on a primary source. You can find these in periodicals and reference books.

Tertiary sources aid the researcher in using primary and secondary sources; these include indexes, dictionaries, guides, and bibliographies.

Nondocumentary sources are unpublished forms of communication and information, which can include conversations with faculty members, other students, and experts in the field.

Discuss sources with your professor before you begin your research, since many instructors may require both primary and secondary sources for your paper.

Getting Started with Topic Development

Has this ever happened to you? You've known all semester long that you have a major research paper due at the end of the term. It's now two weeks before the due date, and for the life of you, you can't think of a topic. Assuming that you come up with a topic soon, you'll have to cram all the research and writing into the last two weeks—on top of studying for finals. If you've been here, you need some techniques for developing a topic.

Sometimes professors assign specific topics for writing assignments or assign a general topic area. Many

Study Stories

"A lot of times, students have a choice of the topic they are going to be writing on. Take time to come up with a topic you really want to learn more about or think would be interesting. Don't just pick a topic for the sake of meeting the due date."

—Micaela H.

other times, however, choosing a topic or narrowing a general topic area to a specific topic is your responsibility.

So how do you choose a topic? Start with a topic that interests you. You'll be much more motivated to write the paper if it captures your interest. Even if the paper is assigned in a class that doesn't interest you, you can probably find a topic related to the class that arouses your interest. Think about the classes that do interest you, and consider whether you can make any connections between those classes and an appropriate topic for this class. Consider the types of books and magazines you are attracted to—any ideas there? Think about your hobbies, interests, and future ambitions. Do they relate to anything you could write about for this class? What about anything currently in the news that you find fascinating—could you turn that into a paper topic?

> **Study Stories**
>
> "I generally come up with an idea and do massive amounts of research before I ever think about writing."
>
> —Sarah P.

Brainstorming is a technique that can help with both developing the topic and organizing the paper itself. Brainstorming is a little like word association; you make a list of everything that you associate with the topic you have in mind.

The cardinal rule of brainstorming is that, in making your initial list, no idea that you associate with your topic is too silly or far-fetched for consideration. Never censor yourself on the first go-'round. Once you've listed 20 or so associations, you can begin to review your list. If you can't come up with 20, chances are you don't yet know enough about the topic to consider it your final selection. However, if you still feel good about the topic, you may want to explore it further before ruling it out.

> **Study Stories**
>
> "I think brainstorming is the key to starting off a good written assignment. I think you have to lay your ideas down before you can make sense of what you are going to write."
>
> —Emily B.

It's often helpful to put your list down after the initial brainstorming and come back to it later. Then scrutinize all the silly and far-fetched associations; do they trigger any realistic ideas or approaches to the topic? If not, cross them off the list. Your edited list can serve as a starting point for developing the topic further, narrowing the topic, and organizing the paper.

In the corporate world, brainstorming is generally conducted in groups—the old "two heads are better than one" notion. You can enlist agreeable friends, roommates, family members, or your instructor in your quest to brainstorm paper ideas. Bounce some ideas off them. Ask for their feedback and contributions. Again, no idea is too ridiculous during the first round of brainstorming. Remember the old adage, "Many a truth is spoken in jest." You never know what gems may be lurking amid ideas that seem truly absurd upon first glance.

Once you've hit upon a topic, be sure it is narrow enough: professors frequently complain that student paper topics are too broad. Don't narrow your topic so much, however, that it will be difficult to find research material on it.

Massage your topic into a research question to guide your exploration of source material. That way, you won't just be amassing disparate facts as you gather your research; you will be conducting an organized search that builds toward addressing your research question. Let's say your topic is the effect of school performance on teen pregnancy. Your research question could be "To what extent does school performance affect teen pregnancy rates?"

Study Suggestions

Don't hesitate to enlist your professor in helping you select and fine-tune your topic. If you've developed your topic with your instructor's assistance, she or he is bound to find it a more interesting paper and view it more favorably in the grading process.

Get more guidance on topic development from these sites: www.library. umw.edu/talon/topic.html, www.uvsc.edu/library/tutorials/ intermediate/topic.html, and http://content.scholastic.com/browse/ article.jsp?id=1593.

Keywords

A major linchpin in your research is the keyword search, which you use to find both library and Internet resources. You likely know something about keyword searches because you probably search the Internet frequently. Two important principles distinguish the keyword searches you'll do for academic assignments.

You must be persistent and creative in using keywords. You can't try just one set of keywords and give up if you get paltry results. An effective keyword search requires a strategy and a list of possible keywords and phrases to try.

Search engines for most academic searches, such as library databases (see the next section), use Boolean searching, named after British mathematician George Boole. This is somewhat different from the searching you may be used to in Internet searches. A Boolean search uses "operators," words that enable you to expand or narrow your search (such as *and, or, not,* and *near*).

Here's a very quick crash course in using Boolean operators:

◆ The search engine looks for an exact phrase if you surround the phrase with quotation marks: "teen pregnancy." This principle is also true of most non-Boolean search engines (such as Google).

◆ If your keyword or phrase (also known as a search term) has commonly used synonyms, the OR operator will enable you to search for the term and its synonyms: teenage OR adolescent.

◆ If you want to narrow your search by having the engine look for documents in which more than one search term appears, use AND as the operator: "teen pregnancy" AND "school performance." In most search engines, you can substitute a plus sign (+) for AND with no space between the + and the subsequent search term: "teen pregnancy" +"school performance."

◆ If you want eliminate a search term that might typically come up in search results for your search term, you can use the NOT operator: "teen pregnancy" NOT abortion. In most search engines, you can substitute a minus sign (–) for NOT with no space between the minus sign and the subsequent search term: "teen pregnancy" –abortion.

◆ To search for words close to each other, but not exact phrases, you can use the NEAR operator: pregnancy NEAR adolescent.

◆ To search for all forms of a word, you can use wildcards by inserting a symbol (usually *, but sometimes % or $) after part of the search word: adolescen* would search for *adolescent* or *adolescence*. pregn* would search for *pregnant* or *pregnancy*. You can also use wildcards to find alternate spellings, such as British and American spellings: lab*r would search for both *labor* and *labour*.

◆ You can use these operators in combination.

Keyword searches using Internet search engines operate on similar but not identical principles. For example, Google generally ignores Boolean operators (and other common words) and is also not case sensitive (that is, it doesn't matter whether the keywords you type are capitalized). But Google does search for exact phrases in quotation marks. You can peruse the nuances of searching the most popular Internet search engines at these URLs:

◆ Google: www.google.com/support/bin/static.
py?page=searchguides.html&ctx=basics

◆ Yahoo: http://help.yahoo.com/l/us/yahoo/search/basics/

◆ Live Search: http://help.live.com/
help.aspx?project=wl_searchv1&mkt=en-us

Study Suggestions _____

You can find complete tutorials on Boolean searches at these sites: http://library.
nyu.edu:8000/research/
tutorials/boolean/boolean.
html; www.gv.psu.edu/
foweb/lib/boolean_search/
index.html; and http://lib.
colostate.edu/tutorials/
boolean.html.

None of this information on keyword searches will help you if you aren't already thinking broadly about your keyword strategy. Consider a few tips for thinking as strategically as possible about your keyword search:

Start brainstorming lists of possible keywords and phrases before you even begin searching. Think about the most important concepts related to your topic. Ask yourself,

"What words would a source have to include to be truly valuable in my search?" Then think about synonyms for the most important words, as well as variations (for example, singular and plural, noun and adjective forms).

It may take the discovery of only one truly relevant article to steer you in the right keyword direction; in most databases, the keywords under which an article is classified are listed with the article. If you look at those keywords for the first really germane article you find, you may get a lot of new ideas for keywords to search for.

Be wary of outdated terms, especially if you are researching a rapidly changing field, such as technology. Enlist your reference librarian in helping you plan your search strategy (see the next section).

Traditional Research Tools

On your college campus is a wonderful building that you may not be very familiar with. It's called the library. Library usage has dropped off dramatically among college students since the Internet became popular. But the library and its personnel remain superlative resources for research. It's true that you can access many of those resources without setting foot in the library, but we recommend that you do explore what your campus library has to offer. Once you know what's available to you, you can make smart judgments about how much you can gain from a physical presence in the library and how many of the library's resources you can access from remote locations, such as your dorm room.

Study Suggestions

Your number-one research ally in the library is the research librarian. Make friends with him or her right away. Research librarians are there to help, and they love to find the answers. They won't do your research for you, but they will steer you in the right direction. A typical question for a research librarian might start out, "Where can I find information about …?" The research librarian can also help with an overall research and keyword strategy.

Now let's look at the major categories of research tools that you can find in the library (many of which you can access from other locations through your campus computer network). Most of these are tertiary sources that will help you identify, find, and use the primary and secondary sources you need for your paper's topic.

Reference books: These specialized publications contain facts compiled from many sources and are organized for quick and easy use. Many are available online either through your campus library or independently through the Internet; some may require a fee.

◆ **Encyclopedias**—These volumes are designed to give you an overview of a topic (and, therefore, are very useful for topic selection and narrowing), including the definition, description, background, and bibliographic references.

◆ **Dictionaries**—These books, of course, contain information about words: meanings, derivation, spelling, pronunciation, syllabication, and usage. Some also contain biographical information, historical information, and pictures or other illustrations. Dictionaries may be useful in the early stages of your research because they yield synonyms that you can use in keyword searches. You can also use them to look up unfamiliar words you come across in your research.

◆ **Yearbooks, handbooks, and almanacs**—Yearbooks are publications issued annually to provide current information in narrative, statistical, or directory form. Handbooks are typically small books that treat broad subjects in brief form and serve as a record of current knowledge. Almanacs are annual calendars containing important dates and statistical information.

◆ **Biographical materials**—Biographical dictionaries contain brief information about the lives of individuals, often describing events that occurred during the time the person lived. Biographies are books that provide the most in-depth information on the lives of persons living or dead.

◆ **Atlases**—An atlas is a collection of maps; however, many atlases also contain descriptive data, demographic information, political history, and economic conditions.

Study Suggestions

Consider interviewing experts as part of your research. This often-overlooked technique will distinguish your paper and impress your professor. You can find experts on your college campus, in the town in which your college is located, or in your hometown. You may also be surprised to discover that many well-known authors, scholars, and authorities are willing to be quoted in your paper. Send them a polite e-mail asking for responses to a couple of questions for a student paper.

Indexes and periodical index databases: These tools provide bibliographic information on articles, essays, speeches, poems, and other written works in periodicals or as collected works. Periodical index databases search magazines, newspapers, and academic journal articles. These indexes and databases cover a wide variety of disciplines. Publishers license these databases to college libraries, and most campuses have licenses for large numbers of databases through which you can access many full-text articles. In some cases, you can access only abstracts of articles (short summaries of the essence of the article), but your library may have the print version of the full article or can order it for you from another library through its interlibrary loan service. While the databases can usually be searched online from remote locations, you generally must go through your campus library's website and enter a username and password to do so. Learn to use these databases because scholarly journals are the gold standard of academic research. Libraries usually offer online tutorials on how to use the databases, and library staff can also help you use them.

Library books and the library catalog: Of course, the library also has thousands of books outside the realm of reference books, and some of them may be valuable in your research. In the library, you can do a computerized search of your library's catalog of holdings, and you can generally conduct such a search on your own computer through your library's website.

Be sure that your research covers a rich variety of *current* sources—books, periodicals, and online sources, as appropriate. A good rule of thumb is that, generally, sources should not be more than 10 years old, unless it would be appropriate to cite older landmark works in your field.

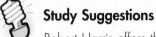

Study Suggestions _____

Robert Harris offers the CARS checklist for evaluating Internet sources (www.virtualsalt/evalu8it.htm):

Credibility: Is the source trustworthy? What are the author's credentials? Is there any evidence of quality control on the site?

Accuracy: Is the source up-to-date? Is it detailed, exact, and comprehensive?

Reasonableness: Does the source seem fair, balanced, objective, and reasoned? Does the tone seem slanted?

Support: Does the site list its sources? Is there contact information so you can ask questions about the source?

Online Searching

Most college students are well acquainted with searching for information on the Internet through such major search engines as Google (www.google.com), Yahoo! (www.yahoo.com), and Live Search (www.live.com). It is certainly possible to search the Internet and find plenty of research material for writing a college paper. However, the quality and trustworthiness of finding the bulk of your research material for a paper that way is highly suspect. Just about anyone can write information and post it on the Internet. What you find, though, often isn't accurate or appropriate for a college paper. That's why the online and offline resources of your library should be the *first* places you explore when conducting research.

Study Suggestions _____

These sites offer valuable criteria for evaluating online sources: http://eduscapes.com/tap/topic32.htm; www.lib.purdue.edu/ugrl/staff/sharkey/interneteval; www.library.ubc.ca/home/evaluating; and http://owl.english.purdue.edu/handouts/research/r_evalsource4.html.

You can use the Internet for ideas for initial topic development and to fill in gaps in your research once you've used library sources. Just be sure to carefully scrutinize anything you find on the Internet to ensure that it's appropriate to cite in your paper.

Following is a small selection of appropriate places to conduct academic research on the Internet. Note that myriad additional helpful reference sites are available, and your campus library's website may offer links to the best of them:

Google Scholar: This specialized version of the widely used Google search engine (http://scholar.google.com) searches academic journal articles. You will likely find, however, that you can't access the vast majority of articles that appear in the search results unless you pay for them. There's a good possibility that you can get the same results by searching your library's databases, through which you probably *can* access the articles at no cost. Starting with your library's databases will likely save time. Using Google Scholar can be advantageous for uncovering articles that you can't find through a library database search. You can then ask your reference librarian how to obtain the article, such as through interlibrary loan. Occasionally, you'll also find an article through Google Scholar that you can access directly, such as through the author's website.

Bartleby.com: Bartleby, at www.bartleby.com, is a huge, easy-to-use collection of reference works—encyclopedias, dictionaries, indexes, fiction and nonfiction books, quotations, and more.

Newspaper and magazine portals: You can access many newspaper and magazine articles at portal sites, such as MagPortal.com (http://magportal.com), FindArticles.com (http://findarticles.com), OnlineNewspapers.com (http://onlinenewspapers.com), and Newslink (http://newslink.com/readnewsletters.html) for newsletters and websites for individual magazines and newspapers. Note that some publishers require a fee for articles.

News sites: You may find it useful to locate current, topical information for your research at sites such as CNN.com (www.cnn.com) and MSN.com (www.msn.com).

Library sites: The Internet Public Library (www.ipl.org), which began in 1995 as a class project, is a huge repository of information, as is the Library of Congress site at www.loc.gov/index.html. Both offer "Ask a Librarian" features. Note that some libraries other than your campus library allow access to their resources and can be perused at sites like Libweb, at http://lists.webjunction.org/libweb.

Using Sources Effectively

One of the hardest aspects of your research will not be finding the information you're looking for, but determining how—or if—you will use all the sources you find. A related issue is how to organize and work with sources.

A tried-and-true method for taking notes about sources is to write each piece of information you think you might use on a 3×5 card along with bibliographic information about the source. These days, you can access so many full-text source materials through your library's databases via its website that you will likely find it more efficient and practical to print articles and highlight the information you feel you might use. Consider using different color highlighters to mark different aspects of your topic. Expenses for paper and printer ink cartridges make this method a bit more costly than taking notes on index cards—and you may also need to pay a nominal fee for printouts if you're printing in the library or a computer lab. To keep the size of the paper containing your research uniform, you may want to make photocopies of sources that you can't print on your computer, such as pages of books—as long as you are not copying so many pages that the cost becomes prohibitive. Write a short evaluation on each printed article about the usefulness of the article to your paper; for example, you could write, "useful for self-esteem aspects of teen-pregnancy issue" or "probably not useful, but don't rule out."

Study Suggestions

Using the Page Setup menu item in the File menu, you can set up your computer's web browser application (Internet Explorer, Safari, or Firefox, for example) to include the information you need on printouts taken from the Internet. For citing online materials, most citation styles require the URL (web address) of the online source and the date of retrieval from the Internet, so be sure you set up your printouts to include that information.

Next, arrange your notes into categories that pertain to various aspects of your topic—that's easy to do if you've color-coded your highlighted articles.

To avoid shuffling through a stack of papers every time you want to insert something from your research into your paper, you might type up all the quotes, paraphrases, summaries, and other information you think you'll likely use in the paper. Then create a separate document for each aspect of your topic and give it a corresponding filename. At this point, the research process begins to overlap with the writing process described in Chapter 12, so also refer to that chapter, especially the sections entitled "Developing a Strategy and Outlining" and "Prewrite-Write-Edit-Revise-Edit-Proofread-Revise." See also the "Research Papers" section in Chapter 13.

Critically evaluate each piece of research. To ensure that your paper is primarily driven by your own ideas, be highly discriminating about your research, using only material that truly supports and adds to your argument. Using the citation style your professor has dictated, begin inserting research material into your paper. Some citation styles call for footnotes or endnotes; others require citations within the text.

The most commonly used academic citation styles are listed here, with web addresses for more information. Note that the most comprehensive guide to each style's rules is contained in an official book about that style, updated every few years. Websites related to each style can give you an overview of the major rules and conventions of the style:

- APA Style (American Psychological Association): www.aresearchguide.com/styleguides.html#3

- Chicago Manual of Style/Turabian Style: www.aresearchguide.com/styleguides.html#4

- CGOS Style—Columbia Guide to Online Style: www.aresearchguide.com/styleguides.html#5

- CBE Style—Council of Biology Editors: www.aresearchguide.com/styleguides.html#6

- Harvard Style: www.aresearchguide.com/styleguides.html#7

- MLA Style (Modern Language Association): www.aresearchguide.com/styleguides.html#8

Also check out Citation Machine at http://citationmachine.net, which enables you to enter information about your sources and see how to format your citation in the style you're using.

Avoiding Plagiarism

When you use ideas, facts, and opinions that are not your own—even when you don't use the author's exact words—you must give appropriate credit to the author as you incorporate his or her ideas into your paper. If you don't do so, you're committing plagiarism, one of the most serious offenses in academia. Virtually every school has an honor code that prohibits plagiarism. Consequences range from failing the assignment or class in which the plagiarism occurred to being expelled from your college.

Plagiarism sometimes results from simple carelessness—for example, overlooking instances in which you should credit the originator of an idea, quote, or phrase that's not yours. More insidious—and more tempting to some students—is downloading or purchasing material that you didn't write and trying to pass it off as your own. Unscrupulous students sometimes paste whole chunks of material into a paper and deliberately fail to credit the source. Or they submit an entire paper downloaded or purchased from one of the plethora of term-paper mills on the Internet.

We caution you strongly not to plagiarize because you will probably get caught. Professors can easily recognize writing that does not read like that of their students. They are also increasingly using sophisticated software and websites that can detect plagiarism. Students who are tempted to plagiarize are usually those who have procrastinated and then find themselves in a bind right before the paper is due. If you are ever in that situation, *talk to your professor immediately* because there is always a better way to deal with your crisis. You may end up having to take a grading penalty for a late paper, but whatever consequence you suffer will be better than the consequence for plagiarizing.

Study Suggestions _____

Consult these sites for more information about avoiding plagiarism:

Plagiarism.org Frequently Asked Questions: http://plagiarism.org/learning_center/plagiarism_faq.html

Plagiarism Prevention for Students: http://turnitin.com/research_site/e_home.html

Avoiding Plagiarism: http://owl.english.purdue.edu/owl/resource/589/01/

Test your knowledge of plagiarism with this plagiarism quiz: www.esc.edu/esconline/across_esc/library.nsf/wholeshortlinks2/Plagiarism+Quiz?opendocument

With that lecture out of the way, we also caution you to avoid unintentional plagiarism caused by carelessness. When in doubt, it's better to overcite than undercite. In other words, any phrases or paraphrases that aren't strictly your own ideas should be credited to their source. You don't need to cite information that is common knowledge, facts and dates available from multiple sources, or words that comprise your own ideas.

Study Stressors _____

One argument against the traditional method of taking notes from your research on 3x5 cards is that you could inadvertently neglect to note that the words you're taking from a source are a direct quote (for example, you could forget to surround the quotation with quotation marks), leading to unintentional plagiarism in your paper. If you use printouts of articles as the basis for the research you insert in your paper, direct quotes will be completely clear to you.

When you use someone else's exact words, use quotation marks around those words and give the author credit using the citation style your professor has indicated. When you paraphrase, give the author credit in the appropriate citation style. If you are not overly dependent on using outside sources, you will be less likely to unintentionally plagiarize. Every citation in your paper must be partnered with a list of sources that typically appears at the end of your paper; this may be titled "Works Cited," "References," "Bibliography," or a similar heading dictated by the citation style you're using. Just as every citation within the paper should correspond to an item on your list of sources, every item on your source list should link to at least one citation in your paper.

What You've Learned

Ready for a quick check to see what you've learned from this chapter? I now understand ...

◆ How to choose and fine-tune a topic for research assignments.

◆ Tricks for performing effective keyword searches.

◆ Ways to use my campus library and reference librarian to aid in my research.

◆ When to use Internet sources in research and how to evaluate their quality.

◆ Techniques for organizing my research notes and incorporating material into my assignments without plagiarizing.

The Least You Need to Know

◆ College students have access to a wealth of research information, but they must approach this information broadly, creatively, and persistently to succeed in topic development, keyword searches, and research.

◆ Research is divided into primary, secondary, tertiary, and nondocumentary sources; students must know which types their professors expect them to use.

◆ Plagiarism is one of the one of the worst offenses in academic life, yet it's one of the easiest to inadvertently commit; thus, students must develop skills in integrating and properly citing their sources.

Chapter 12

Writing Essentials

In This Chapter

- ◆ Learn about typical student writing struggles
- ◆ Grasp techniques for planning and executing papers
- ◆ Develop awareness of common student writing flaws
- ◆ Discover methods to overcome writing difficulties

For many students, writing is the most difficult part of attaining academic success. Some have little difficulty with tests and other assignments but suffer major angst and fear over writing.

Student writing traumas lead to several typical situations. There's the student who knows for weeks that a paper is due but finds the idea of writing it so agonizing that procrastination sets in. And the student who lacks motivation to write after being assigned a boring topic by an instructor. And the student who has conducted so much research that he or she doesn't know where to begin and how to organize the paper. Lastly, there's the student who finally overcomes procrastination and writes the assigned paper, but has put it off so long that it is literally hot off the printer when handed to the teacher—and certainly not edited or proofed. Any of these sound a bit too familiar to you?

This chapter will help you avoid these situations by leading you through the process of effectively tackling a typical writing assignment—in this case, a paper that you learned how to research in Chapter 11.

Developing a Strategy and Outlining

You can fend off a significant amount of the panic that often accompanies a writing assignment by developing a strategy for your paper and then preparing an outline.

Strategy

Developing a strategy is the simplest way of organizing a writing assignment.

Study Suggestions

Developing a writing strategy for a paper works best in a conducive environment, in which you have a clear mind and a quiet, comfortable situation to nurture the planning process. Don't panic if nothing jumps into your head immediately; if you relax, ideas should start to gel in your mind.

As you develop a strategy for your paper, you engage in the mental process of picturing the finished product in your head. Conjuring a mental image of your paper will reassure you: your paper exists—all you have to do is transfer that mental image to words on paper. You don't have to write anything down in the strategy-development process, but you certainly can do so if it helps you.

Some of the strategic questions you may want to think about as your paper takes shape in your mind include these:

How long should it be? This question may already be answered by your instructor's assignment, but you'll want to think about whether it will be difficult to write as much as assigned or to confine yourself to the assigned length. If you anticipate problems with length, ask about your instructor's policy on too-short and too-long papers.

Will you cite outside sources in your paper, hence requiring some form of bibliography? Will you want to prepare any charts, tables, graphs, or illustrations? How long will they take?

What will the paper's title be? If you can conceptualize a title, you'll have an excellent starting point for writing the paper. (Bear in mind that some instructors prefer that you not title your papers; if that's the case, title it in your head even though it won't have a title on paper.) Another way to jump-start the strategy process is to imagine your paper is a newspaper story. What should its headline be?

How will you begin the paper? How will you state your thesis?

In what order will you express your supporting points? What organizational scheme will best bolster your thesis?

Think about your audience—generally your instructor. What is he or she looking for? Are the professor's instructions for the assignment clear?

Include your professor in your strategy process. Most instructors will be only too happy to make research suggestions, check your bibliography, go over your outline, and even look over your rough draft. Discussing your paper with the instructor shows him or her that you care about doing a good job. Even if your paper ends up being less than he or she hoped for, chances are the instructor will give you at least some benefit of the doubt when it comes to grading simply because he or she knows you tried hard to write a successful paper. However, don't wait until just a few days before the due date to approach your professor about the paper for the first time. The prof will be much less inclined to lend a hand if you approach him or her at the eleventh hour having done little or nothing!

> **Study Stories**
>
> "When in doubt, talk with the professor. If I'm really struggling with something, I'll talk with the professor to see if I'm on the right track. Usually the professors will ask you questions to get you thinking and head you in the right direction."
>
> —Stephanie G.

One aspect of developing a writing strategy is to break the writing assignment into smaller chunks and devise a timetable.

Let's say your semester begins September 1, and you receive a syllabus detailing an assignment for a major research paper due December 1. Here's how you might set up your timetable:

Sept. 1	Receive assignment
Sept 1 to Sept. 15	Develop and finalize topic
Sept. 15 to Oct. 15	Conduct research
Oct. 15 to Oct. 30	Do preliminary bibliography
Oct. 30 to Nov. 5	Do outline
Nov. 5 to Nov. 15	Write first draft
Nov. 15 to Dec. 1	Edit, revise, proofread, and polish final draft; finalize bibliography

Study Stories

"Start early. Having a timeline planned out can help. For example, set a goal to have a certain number of pages done by a certain day before the paper is due."

—Heather A.

Study Stressors

The poorly structured paper frequently results from procrastinating and failing to plan adequately. If you take the time to develop a strategy, the major points of your paper will flow logically from each other and build upon each other. In short, your paper will make sense.

Outlining

You've known about outlining at least since middle school and probably elementary school. Indeed, the very fact that you were taught to outline from an early age may prompt you to resist the technique when it comes to your college papers. Outlining can be a faithful old friend to college writers, however, and one that will serve you especially well when you write longer papers.

The outline is an organizational framework, the skeleton of your paper to which you will add the flesh. The outline can help you fight the college-writing flaw that instructors cite as their number-one pet peeve: poor organization. A good outline serves as a road map that enables you to visualize where your paper is headed. If a point seems out of place in an outline, chances are it will be even more so in your paper, and your instructor will notice immediately.

Study Stories

"Always start with a general outline to gather your ideas ... anything on a scratch of paper will work. If there is time, you can consult with your teacher and other students. If you are writing at the last minute in a panic, an outline helps to guide your thinking and keeps your paper from going off on pointless tangents."
—Adrianne W.

Since you undoubtedly already know a lot about outlining, we won't spend much time here discussing the how-to's of the technique. You should know, however, that there's more than one way to outline, so adapt the one that works best for you. You may even want to change formats from paper to paper or start out with a rough outline and work your way up to the more thorough sentence outline.

The basic types of outlines include these:

♦ Rough or working outline

♦ Topic outline

♦ Sentence outline

The rough or working outline is an informal blueprint that may not even be in traditional outline form.

Study Stories

"Write an outline first. It was usually harder for me to sit down and start writing without knowing where my paper was going. My outline was a roadmap, and I could anticipate the end of the paper."
—Micaela H.

The topic outline follows traditional outline form but uses topics and subtopics, expressed as simple words or phrases, for each entry.

Obviously, the sentence outline uses complete sentences for each entry. The sentence outline is the most formal of organizational techniques and the one that will probably bear the closest relationship to your final paper.

> **Study Suggestions**
>
> Microsoft Word, the word-processing program that most students use, offers outlining tools. Choose Outline in the View menu.

The sentence outline supports the organizational process by forcing you to think through the structure of your paper. Whereas the topic outline structures the general concepts you will write about, the sentence outline organizes what you will say about each concept or topic.

Building and Using Your Vocabulary

A common complaint among college professors is that student writing lacks the sophistication and level of vocabulary expected of college students.

The thesaurus feature that comes with Microsoft Word and other word-processing programs is a godsend for students with underdeveloped vocabularies. A thesaurus in print form can't hurt, either.

> **Study Suggestions**
>
> Building your vocabulary has many advantages beyond improving your writing. A rich, well-developed vocabulary will make you a better contributor to class discussions, a better reader, and a learner who can make connections among various disciplines.

Techniques that actually help you to *learn* new words and build your vocabulary will be more useful to you in the long run, however. Now it probably does not sound practical to drop everything in the middle of writing a paper to improve your vocabulary—and it's not. But you can employ techniques while writing your paper to boost your command of words.

Research shows that one of the best vocabulary builders is reading— and you will certainly do a lot of reading while researching your paper. Make it a habit to jot down unfamiliar words you come across while researching your paper and learn their definitions and usage. Consider keeping a file of new words on 3×5 cards with definitions and examples of how to use them in a sentence. Use some of these new words in your paper.

Punctuation and Grammar

College professors expect a certain level of writing competence from their students. That competence is embodied in how clearly students organize, express, and support their ideas in writing, but professors also judge writing proficiency based on your proper use of punctuation and grammar.

Not only are correct grammar and punctuation crucial required components of the overall writing package you present to your instructor, but their incorrect use simply makes your paper much harder to read. Imagine your textbooks loaded with typos, misspellings, faulty punctuation, and poor grammar. You'd find them much more difficult to read because your brain would have to pause frequently to figure out what the author was really trying to say. That's how professors feel when reading a sloppy paper, and their disdain cannot possibly help your grade.

Based on survey research we've conducted with college professors, we know that the following top the list of writing errors that irritate instructors and result in lower grades:

Misspellings and typos/sloppiness: Typos and misspellings are especially annoying to teachers because they are so easily avoidable. A paper riddled with misspelled words signals a lack of care and certainly a lack of proofreading. Use your spell checker and be sure to allow enough time to spell-check before turning in your paper.

Just what is the difference between a typo and a misspelling, anyway? A misspelling is a word that you deliberately write or type incorrectly because you don't know the correct spelling, while a typo is a word that you may know perfectly well how to spell, but you mistype it so that

Study Stressors

One of the worst typos we've seen in a college paper—that was not caught by a spell-checker—was *plattow*, when the writer clearly meant *plateau*.

it appears as a misspelled word—or the wrong word. With that in mind, it's important to remember that spell checkers will not catch a word that is spelled correctly but is not the correct word for the context. For example, we frequently mistype *from* as *form*. *Form* is spelled correctly, but its meaning is very different from the meaning of *from*. That's where careful proofreading comes in.

While spell-checking is key to catching most misspellings, thorough proofing is essential for catching the misspellings that appear as out-of-context words, as well as for spotting typos and sloppiness.

Awkward or confusing sentence structure: You can usually simplify by breaking a sentence into two or more sentences and by ensuring that all modifiers (adjectives and adverbs) and clauses (groups of related words that contain both a subject and a predicate, and that function as part of a sentence) are structurally close to the elements to which they refer. You can also cut out unnecessary clauses and phrases (groups of related words without a subject and a predicate that function as a single part of speech). When you can join two sentences gracefully and without adding confusion, by all means join them. But if compound subjects, compound verbs, and numerous clauses have obscured the meaning of your sentences, it may be time to simplify.

Sentence fragments: Sentences need to have a subject and a verb. If a sentence does not have both, it's a fragment, which you can frequently successfully attach to another sentence. Consider the sentence you just read. A clumsy student might write: "If a sentence does not have both, it's a fragment. Which you can frequently successfully attach to another sentence." The student can perform a quick fix by turning the sentence fragment into a clause, setting it off with a comma, and attaching it to the sentence to which it belongs. Make sure all your sentences have both a subject and a verb, and when appropriate, perform reattachment surgery on these that don't.

Run-on sentences: Think of the run-on sentence as the evil twin of the sentence fragment. Where the sentence fragment lacks a subject or verb, the run-on sentence has too many of both. There's nothing wrong with joining two sentences into one compound sentence, as long as you use an appropriate connector between the two sentences. An appropriate connector is either a conjunction (such as *and, but, yet, so, however*) or punctuation (such as a semicolon or colon, but *not* a comma). Joining two complete sentences with a comma results in the most common type of run-on sentence.

> **Study Stories**
>
> "I think that grammar is so important; you have to make sure that you at least sound intelligent through what you write."
>
> —Emily B.

Incorrect word usage: You may remember all those confusing pairs: *affect* and *effect, less* and *fewer, among* and *between, farther* and *further, lay* and *lie, who* and *whom, that* and *which, principle* and *principal* ... the list goes on and on. For a concise and handy reference on word usage, obtain a copy of Strunk and White's *The Elements of Style*, available in an inexpensive paperback, and read and refer to the chapter called "Words and Expressions Commonly Misused" (or access it at www. bartleby.com/141/strunk3.html). The entire book is valuable to the student writer who wants to earn better grades, but the chapter on word usage is particularly useful.

Be aware, too, that the word-usage flaws that especially drive professors off the deep end are the simplest ones that everyone should know to avoid: *to, too,* and *two; there, their,* and *they're; it's* and *its*. The only time *it's* is used with an apostrophe is when it is a contraction for "it is." If you learn no other correct word usage, at least learn these easy rules.

Be wary of these other sets in your writing:

- Assure, ensure, insure
- Awhile, while
- Capital, capitol
- Complement, compliment
- Compose, comprise

- Counsel, council

- Continual, continuous

- Flammable, inflammable

- Imply, infer

- Respective, respectively

- Stationary, stationery

Punctuation problems: Improper or nonuse of punctuation marks, especially commas, can greatly hamper your paper's readability. Few substitutes exist for simply knowing the rules. If you don't know them, you can refer to a good grammar book or use a grammar checker on your computer. Think of punctuation marks as traffic signs that tell you to stop or pause. If your paper lacks the appropriate stops and pauses, it probably won't read well and will benefit from periods, commas, and other punctuation.

Poor or nonexistent transitions: College papers often lack flow because students have made little or no effort to connect paragraphs. Since this problem relates to poor organization, improving your paper's organization will set the scene for improved transitions.

Study Suggestions

Several websites list transition words and devices commonly used to improve writing flow:

http://larae.net/write/transition.html

www.studygs.net/wrtstr6.htm

http://jc-schools.net/write/transition.htm

http://owl.english.purdue.edu/owl/resource/574/01/

Wordiness: Student writers often use more words than are necessary to express your ideas, often rendering sentences too complex and papers too long. As you edit and revise your paper, scrutinize the necessity of every word. Have you used more words than needed? What words can you eliminate without changing the meaning of your sentences? Every word should contribute to your point. If "it goes without saying," why say it? As a longtime professor of freshman composition writes: "Think of each sentence in your paper as a snapshot on a roll of film; normally only a few will be worth keeping." Avoid the wordy phrases that typically ensnare student writers: "in an attempt to" (can usually be eliminated), "in order to" (*to* is usually adequate), "on a daily (weekly, monthly, annual, regular) basis" (*daily, weekly, annually, regularly*), "due to the fact that" (*because*).

Nonagreement of subject and verb: Singular subjects must take singular verbs, and plural subjects take plural verbs. It's a fairly easy problem to avoid with simple sentences, but it can be harder to detect in more complex sentences:

Wrong: Every student, especially seniors, know the cafeteria's hours.

Right: Every student, especially seniors, knows the cafeteria's hours.

Grammar books and grammar checkers can provide shortcuts if you don't have a firm grasp of this grammatical concept.

Nonagreement of noun and pronoun: When you use a pronoun to refer to a noun you've already used, the pronoun must agree in number with the noun.

Wrong: When a student wants to add a course, they must have a slip signed by an adviser.

Right: When a student wants to add a course, he or she must have a slip signed by an adviser.

Study Stressors _____

Other common student writing flaws that surveyed professors cited as damaging to good student writing include these errors (see the associated web references for more information on avoiding these errors):

Vague pronoun reference: http://owl.english.purdue.edu/owl/resource/595/01/

Inappropriate use of passive voice: http://owl.english.purdue.edu/owl/resource/539/01/

Short, choppy sentences and/or paragraphs: http://owl.english.purdue.edu/owl/resource/573/03/

Dangling clauses/phrases: http://owl.english.purdue.edu/owl/resource/597/01/

Lack of parallelism: http://owl.english.purdue.edu/owl/resource/623/01/

Incorrect use of restrictive and nonrestrictive clauses: www.kentlaw.edu/academics/lrw/grinker/LwtaClauses__Restrictive_and_Nonrest.htm

Five-Paragraph Formula

If you're an insecure college writer, you can benefit from following a writing formula that you can apply to many situations. That way, you always know exactly how to approach almost any writing situation. You can avoid considerable procrastination and fear because you have a step-by-step plan that enables you to plunge right into writing the piece.

This formula works best for shorter assignments, such as essays and papers written over a relatively short period that don't require enormous amounts of research. The principles can be applied to the long research paper, but the basic building blocks of the formula are five paragraphs. In essence, the formula expands on the idea of the outline; if you take the main sentence from each paragraph, you should have a coherent outline.

Study Stories

"What helps me is making lists of things I want to include in each paragraph. I do research on each of the main points and eliminate or add to the lists based on my findings. Then I take my main paragraphs and write them out. By writing out the main paragraphs, I have a good idea of what the main point of my paper is going to be (for the introduction paragraph) and what conclusions I want to make at the very end."
—Jessica W.

The five-paragraph formula is as follows:

Paragraph 1: Introduction, a three-part thesis statement

Paragraph 2: Supporting argument for first point in thesis statement

Paragraph 3: Supporting argument for second point in thesis statement

Paragraph 4: Supporting argument for third point in thesis statement

Paragraph 5: Conclusion and implications

To expand on the formula for longer pieces, simply write as many subheadings and paragraphs as necessary for each part of the formula. Here's an example of the introduction and topic sentences for subsequent paragraphs in a paper written according to the five-paragraph formula:

Paragraph 1: If Americans intend to solve the nation's garbage crisis, they must learn the Three R's: Recycle, Reduce, and Reuse.

Paragraph 2: Recycling involves not only recycling products and packaging, such as bottles and cans, but also buying products made from recycled materials.

Paragraph 3: The average American throws away an average of 500 pounds of garbage annually; compare this figure to the average European, who tosses less than half that amount annually.

Paragraph 4: Reusing involves saving containers, such as cardboard boxes, and reusing them for other purposes.

Paragraph 5: The nation's trash and landfill crisis can be solved only if all Americans actively get involved in the Three R's: Recycling, Reusing, and Reducing. By working together, we can solve this crisis.

Prewrite-Write-Edit-Revise-Edit-Proofread-Revise

Educators and writing experts advise student writers—and, indeed, all writers—to follow this seven-step plan for producing any piece of writing.

Prewriting: In addition to getting you started on writing your paper, prewriting can spark your interest. Write about the topic before you even do any research about it. This prewriting should have the effect of motivating your research and shaping your thinking about the topic. The exercise will help you develop an effective approach to the topic. The prewriting needn't be a major, time-consuming project; it can be as little as a page or so of rough writing and/or notes.

Your prewriting should consist of three components:

1. What you already know about the topic

2. How you feel about the topic

3. Your predictions for what you think your research will prove

Writing what you already know about the topic is very much like brainstorming. Simply list everything you can think of about this topic.

> **Study Stories** _____
>
> "Just start writing whatever comes to mind about the topic, and then go over it and fix it as you go along. The hardest part is starting it, so that's how I deal with it. I don't think too much before I write. I start to think when I'm in the middle of writing. I do a lot of rearranging, cutting and pasting, and deleting when I write."
>
> —Sabrina O.

Next write about your feelings on the topic. Jot down any preconceived notions, biases, or opinions you may have about the subject. Write down any personal memories associated with the topic. If you didn't develop the topic yourself, speculate on why you think your professor assigned you this topic.

> **Study Stories** _____
>
> "A lot of times, I just write what I feel. Teachers like your opinion, and if you can find something from the reading or research that relates specifically to your life, they like it even more because it allows you to take ownership of your work. I write things that I want others to read, not things that I have to write because the teacher said so."
> —Laura B.

Finally, make some educated guesses on the conclusions that your research will lead to. Hypothesize what the arguments will be and which ones will prevail. Predict how your paper will turn out.

During the prewriting process, ensure that you know who your audience is—generally, your instructor—and think about how you will meet your audience's requirements. The prewriting phase is a good time to decide how you will limit your topic and decide what your thesis statement will be.

Writing: In the writing phase, draw from your prewriting and follow your outline to construct the first draft of your paper. Let your assignment guide you—what type of paper has your professor asked you to write? (See some of the possibilities in Chapter 13.) Write a compelling opening paragraph that entices the reader and coherently states your thesis or main point. Ensure that you've logically arrived at your conclusion and that you've expressed it well.

Pay close attention to properly citing the sources you quote using the citation style your instructor has asked you use. You may find it easier to construct your bibliography (also called a "References" or "Works Cited" section) as you arrive at places in your paper where you are quoting from one of your sources—rather than save the tedious bibliography for the end.

> **Study Suggestions** _____
>
> You may find if helpful to write more than the minimum and then edit down. Say your professor requires a certain number of words. Consider in your first draft writing several hundred more than that. It's always easier to trim out excess fat than it is to try to come up with substantial and well-written arguments if the paper is too skimpy.

Study Suggestions _____

Time is at a premium in writing a college paper. Yet some college students still make the writing process twice as long as it needs to be by first composing their papers in longhand and then typing them. Essentially, they do double the work. Old habits die hard. If you've always composed in longhand before typing, you may find it difficult to break out of the routine. If you can learn to cut the two-step process down to one, however, you can save yourself enormous amounts of time. If you're unaccustomed to composing on your computer, you will likely benefit from a road map, such as an outline.

Editing: In the editing phase, read primarily for content (but make a note of faulty mechanics you spot) and identify what's good about the paper. Signal all the cogent, well-written passages with a mark in the margin.

Study Stories _____

"Reread your paper multiple times. You can almost always find a way to improve the paper. Have at least one or two people read your paper before you are done. It is good to hear other people's opinion because teachers will have a different opinion from your own."

—Amber J.

Scrutinize your thesis statement and ensure that you've presented all those good passages in an order that supports your thesis. At this point, you may notice that you've left out important arguments or details that would bolster your premise.

Revising: Insert missing pieces into an almost-final draft using all your best passages and new arguments in logical order. Where necessary, construct or improve transitions to get you smoothly from one passage to the next.

Editing: Having inserted your edits, read the revised draft aloud or into a tape-recorder and play it back. Watch for when you run out of breath in reading a sentence; that sentence is probably too long and complex. Reading aloud is a great way to flag awkward constructions, bumpy sentences, missing transitions and punctuation, and just plain murky writing.

Study Stories _____

"I always print out the paper and come back to it the next day and reread it. That is the easiest way for me to catch my own mistakes. I have to give my eyes a break from it, and if I just wrote it, I think it looks perfect. But if I look at it a day later, I almost always find grammatical errors or phrases and sentences I just want to reword."
—Sarah P.

Proofread: Finally, read your paper one more time with an eye toward spelling and grammatical errors and correct those errors. Most of us are notoriously bad proofreaders of our own work. Thus, the more distance we can put between ourselves and our writing, the better proofreaders we'll be. One of the best ways to achieve this distance is to allow enough time to proofread your paper once, put it down overnight (longer, if your schedule allows), and then take a fresh look at it the next day—or better yet, ask a friend to view it with fresh eyes.

Study Suggestions _____

Be sure you know how your instructor prefers written assignments to be "packaged." Is a cover page required? Does the professor like report covers? What about margins, fonts, page numbers, and headings? Some teachers are so particular about these requirements that you can hurt your grade if you fail to follow instructions. Most professors at least want you to staple your paper. We can't tell you how many students have asked us when turning in assignments, "Do you have a stapler?" Our response: "Would you ask your boss for a stapler when handing in an important report?"

What You've Learned

Ready for a quick check to see what you've learned from this chapter? I now understand ...

◆ How to get started with planning and writing papers.

◆ The writing flaws that most irritate professors.

- How to structure a paper to make it effective.

- The process of writing and revising that results in a paper worthy of a good grade.

The Least You Need to Know

- While many college students fear writing assignments, they can succeed with writing by developing a strategy and outlining their papers before beginning.

- College professors cite several common writing flaws they see in student papers; students can write more effective papers by learning how to avoid these typical errors.

- Successful papers result from allowing sufficient time to execute a process of prewriting, writing, editing, revising, and proofreading.

Chapter 13

Academic Papers and Other Written Assignments

In This Chapter

- ◆ Learn about the most commonly assigned college papers
- ◆ Understand how to structure each type of paper
- ◆ Get ideas on how to develop paper topics
- ◆ Discover common pitfalls with each type of paper

You will encounter many different types of writing assignments in your college career, so it helps to go into your college classes prepared for all the nuances of "the college paper." Our aim in this chapter is to give you an overview of the major categories of assignments that may come your way and offer some suggestions on how you might approach each type.

College papers are subject to a variety of terminologies, and not all professors use the terms to mean the same things. As we define them, *paper* and *term paper* mean the same thing. An *essay* is generally a piece of writing about another piece of writing or groups of writings, or on a specific topic without the use of outside sources. Some professors might substitute the word *theme*. A *research paper* is any paper that uses sources beyond a primary source. Whereas an essay about a piece of writing would deal only with your own thoughts about the piece of writing (using passages from the writing itself to support your ideas), a research paper about a piece of writing would include your thoughts about the piece of writing and also thoughts expressed by others in secondary sources (literary criticism, for example). When applied to literature or other writing, a research paper may also be an *original-argument paper using sources* or a *literary research paper*.

Be sure you know how your professors define these terms before you tackle assignments. Also be sure before beginning any writing assignment that you understand what *your* professor requires and expects. You may even want to ask if you can view sample successful writing assignments from past students.

Expository Essays and Reports

Outside of creative writing—fiction, poetry, short stories, plays, and the like—expository writing is the major umbrella term for most college writing assignments, and many variations fall within the umbrella. In the most simplistic terms, an expository paper is one that explains. Edward Proffitt defines expository writing in the glossary of his *Reading and Writing about Literature* as "writing designed to explain something in a clear, concise manner. [Expository] essays, which may support a theme or argue a thesis, are aimed at communicating thoughts with clarity, and ideally, with pleasure." An expository essay can explain the views of others (such as other writers, as in *expository essays about literature*); report on an event, situation, or subject (such as in *descriptive* and *narrative essays*); present and summarize a topic in detail (such as in a *report*); compare and contrast two or more works or two or more of anything (as in a *comparative essay*); or argue for a certain position (as in an *argumentative essay*).

A large portion of expository writing in college consists of writing about other writing. In English composition and literature classes, you'll do expository writing about writings in those disciplines. In business and communication classes, you'll write expositorily from sources that may include writing but may encompass others as well.

Although professors will sometimes ask for expository papers summarizing other works, most assigned exposition is analytical. You are expected to examine and interpret components or aspects (such as plot, character, setting, theme, tone, or style) of units of writing. You may be asked to place readings into a larger context of other works in the field.

Breaking the work into components or aspects is the key to analysis. Analysis differentiates elements of the text and then describes the importance of each element to understand the work as a whole. Your writing should unfold in a way that makes your reasoning easy to follow and that demonstrates how you conducted your analysis and reached your conclusions.

Study Stressors

In assigning an expository paper that requires analysis, your professor may expect you to detect something particularly distinctive about the work you're analyzing. It's therefore a good idea to check in with the professor as your paper progresses to ensure that you're on the right track.

In addition to analytical treatments, your professor might assign you to take one of these approaches to expository writing:

◆ **Explication:** A narrower analysis of a work (often poetry) requiring examination and interpretation of components or aspects of comparatively small units of writing, such as paragraphs, lines, sentences, or words.

◆ **Response:** Your own personal reaction to a work and how it connects to your own experience, thoughts, and ideas.

◆ **Evaluation:** A step beyond a response essay; a judgment about a work, generally about whether the work is effective or meets certain standards.

◆ **Synthesis:** An essay that shows how two or more works—or two or more components or aspects of one or more works—are connected, without taking the further step of comparing and contrasting the works or parts of works.

◆ **Process:** An essay that describes, step by step, how to do something (for example, how to succeed at a certain video game).

While the form of expository writing known as the report is primarily the province of elementary, middle, and high school (because reports generally do not require the higher-order thinking skills expected in college), college professors sometimes assign reports. A report is an organized collection of information on a single topic. You may gather information from one or more primary sources, but your professor will probably direct you to secondary sources.

Study Suggestions

The following is an effective way to structure a report:

Introduction, identifying the question you're answering, topic you're summarizing, and reading you've read.

Summary of the most relevant information about the topic, organized logically.

Brief conclusion, providing highlights of the summary.

Study Stressors

Because you don't have the creative latitude afforded by asserting and defending your own argument, summarizing information for a report in your own words may be difficult. (Remember in grade school when you used the encyclopedia and struggled to write the information in your own words?) The ability to paraphrase is paramount in report writing.

The professor's objective in assigning a report is usually content driven. He or she wants you to answer a specific question, find out about a given topic, or show that you've absorbed a certain reading. This is the instructor's way of helping you learn or study about a particular subject. Writing skills are as important as with any other type of writing, but content is likely your instructor's most important grading criterion.

Descriptive Essays

A descriptive essay describes a specific subject—a person, place, thing, or event, for example. Professors often assign descriptive essays because description is one of the building blocks of other types of expository writing. The key to a descriptive essay is to enable a reader to experience whatever you're describing with the same sensory vividness that you, as the writer, experienced it.

You must have a purpose in mind—something you are striving to get across—with your descriptive essay. Yes, one purpose is that your professor has assigned you this essay, but what main idea do you want to communicate about the person, place, object, experience, or memory you are describing? What makes the subject of your essay important or significant? Let's say you choose to describe your sister. Should your purpose be to show that she is an accomplished horseback rider or to illustrate how she relates to other people? That's your choice, but your purpose in writing the description will guide you in which details you choose to include in your essay. Those details should not only support your purpose, but also convey a clear, dominant impression on the reader.

An effective way to develop descriptive details is to conduct a simple word-association exercise with the subject you're describing. Think of as many words as you can come up with that you associate with the subject. The first words that come to you will likely be the most obvious, but keep brainstorming to list words that go beyond those that you might normally use to describe your subject. Use some words from this exercise to build the details of your description. While you can certainly write a descriptive essay from memory, it may help you to choose a subject that you can actually observe as you're planning the paper—a location on campus, your roommate, or the contents of your backpack, for example.

Strive to include a complete sensory experience for your reader, encompassing all five senses. Consider the subject you are describing. What does it look like, smell like, sound like, taste like, or feel like? Write down the five senses—sight, hearing, smell, taste, sound—and see if you can develop a detail about your subject for each. (It won't always be possible to do so; for example, it would be difficult to use taste when describing a person.) Consider the word choices you might use to make something very ordinary sound extraordinary.

> ### Study Stressors
>
> The flaw in descriptive writing that experts cite most frequently is that it *tells* instead of *shows*. Use specific details to show the aspects of your description rather than merely telling it.
>
> *Sentence that tells:* My sister is a smoker.
>
> *Sentence that shows:* When I picture my sister, it is with a cigarette perched between nicotine-stained fingers, her mouth spewing streams of smoke intermingled with barking coughs, and ashes perpetually plummeting from the cigarette's end to objects below.

Provide additional details about what you are describing by asking yourself a series of questions: What is the context or setting of what I'm describing? What really sticks out in my mind about what I'm describing? What does the subject of my description remind me of? What can I compare the subject of my essay to? What are the unusual or extraordinary characteristics of what I'm describing? How do I feel about the subject I'm describing? (Note that, depending on your professor's instructions, you don't have to take a subjective, feeling approach to your subject; you can offer an entirely detached, objective approach.) What do I want my reader to feel about it? What words would best grab the reader's attention and communicate what I want the reader to experience? You may also want to ask yourself the classic questions of journalism: who what, where, when, why, and how.

Common approaches to a descriptive essay include describing the subject in terms of all five senses, describing it based on its location or surroundings, describing the subject (such as a journey) chronologically from beginning to end, or describing it using a then-and-now approach (such as farmland on which you played as a child that has now become a housing development).

Study Suggestions

The following is an effective way to structure a descriptive essay:

Introduction, which moves from general to specific and contains a thesis statement setting forth the dominant impression to be conveyed to the reader and touching on the main points to be described.

Main body, in which each paragraph offers a single descriptive aspect of your subject and supports the dominant impression to be conveyed to the reader.

Three or more paragraphs (depending on your professor's guidelines), each describing a specific aspect.

Conclusion, in which you restate your thesis statement in another way.

Ensure that you have done as much as you can with your descriptive essay by reviewing it against this checklist:

◆ Have you included sufficient convincing detail to enable your reader to envision or experience whatever you are describing?

◆ Have you included details that don't belong and can be omitted?

◆ Have you strived to show and not just tell?

◆ Have you varied your words and used vivid and concrete language?

◆ Does the order in which you've presented the details build your description in a way that best creates an experience for your reader?

◆ Is your description interesting?

Narrative Essays

A narrative essay essentially tells a story. A good way to think of a narrative essay is to consider a variation on the word *narrative—narrator—* and think of yourself as the narrator of a story of someone's experience (probably yours). Professors often assign students to write narrative essays about their own experiences. Some students find writing about themselves quite easy and natural, while others become unhinged at the idea of having to chronicle their own experiences. Students often think nothing in their lives is story-worthy; if you are one of those, consider these prompts for narrative essays:

♦ My most memorable …

♦ How I got interested in …

♦ How I achieved …

♦ How I failed at …

♦ How I realized …

♦ My most frightening experience …

♦ My best experience with …

♦ My worst experience with …

♦ My happiest time …

♦ My first experience with …

♦ The weirdest …

♦ My favorite …

♦ How I handled … (for example, change, conflict, danger, uncertainty)

As you can see, thinking about firsts, bests, worsts, and mosts will help you develop a topic if your professor hasn't assigned one.

Most narrative essays are written in first person (I), so another way to jump-start your thinking about your topic is to write *I* followed by a verb (*saw, felt, wept, went, smiled,* or *wanted,* for example) and see if that simple phrase sparks any thoughts of experiences to write about. One more way to find narrative-essay topics and also see excellent examples of narrative essays is to scan *Reader's Digest,* a magazine that is probably available in your library (or go to www.rd.com/stories). Another source for examples is the radio show "This American Life," which you can hear on National Public Radio (you can also download it from www.thisamericanlife.org or purchase it from iTunes).

As in a descriptive essay, a narrative essay should draw the reader into the experience you are narrating, essentially re-creating the experience for the reader. It should also contain sensory details the way a descriptive essay does. Finally, as in the descriptive essay, the essay should offer a central theme, point, or purpose, creating for the reader a dominant impression—often an observation, insight, or universal truth about human nature or the human condition. Sometimes the story's purpose is even a lesson learned or a moral (as in, "the moral of the story is ...").

Study Stressors

Experts caution that not all narrative essays are written as stories, citing book reports as prime examples of narrative essays *not* written in story form. If your professor assigns a book report, you can be fairly certain that it should not be written as a story. But if you are assigned another type of narrative essay, be sure to ask if it's not clear whether your professor wants a story format.

Beyond what you would find in a descriptive essay, however, a narrative essay contains the elements you find in story writing: plot, character, point of view, climax, and ending. Often an element of conflict is also present, and the narrative essay may include dialogue. Weaving together these experiential elements are details that support the point of the story and move it forward.

Study Suggestions

An effective way to structure a narrative essay is as follows:

Introductory paragraph, setting up the type of story you will be telling and hinting at the purpose or point of the story. Setting and characters may be introduced in this paragraph or in one that follows shortly.

Middle paragraphs, offering event-driven and/or character-driven description and details that move the plot forward and build toward the climax.

Climax.

Conclusion, explicating the purpose or point of the story.

Because narrative essays usually involve personal reflections, emotions, and experiences, they especially lend themselves to prewriting (see Chapter 12). If you have a topic for your narrative essay but still feel uncomfortable about writing about yourself, think about the many ways you tell stories in everyday life by talking on the phone and in person with friends and family. You probably also write stories regularly through e-mail, instant messaging, and even texting. If thinking about those experiences still doesn't loosen you up, consider telling your story to a tape recorder before you write it. Or write about the experience in a stream-of-consciousness manner until the story structure begins to emerge. Because stories unfold in a specific sequence, your narrative essay also will benefit from your having constructed an outline before you write.

Comparative Essays

A comparative essay points out the similarities or differences in two or more works or two or more components or aspects of one or more works (or two or more authors, two or more theories, two or more historical figures, two or more works of art—in fact, two or more of anything). Since comparisons are important building blocks of research papers and other college writing, professors often assign comparative essays as practice for other genres.

Clearly, when you are writing a comparative essay, it is crucial that you completely grasp both of the items you are comparing. You also need a frame of reference for comparison. As Kerry Walk of Harvard University's Writing Center notes, the frame of reference could be an idea, theme, question, problem, or theory. For example, in comparing two twentieth-century artists, painter Alice Neel and photographer Diane Arbus, the frame of reference could be that both women captured in their art the *zeitgeist* of the experience of mid-century American women.

Next, you need grounds for comparison—in other words, what is your rationale for choosing the items you're comparing? In the example of Alice Neel and Diane Arbus, the grounds for comparison could include the facts that both women were producing art at about the same time, and they were both portraitists (who even portrayed some of the same people).

Typically, Walk says, you'll use transition words and phrases, such as *similarly, moreover, on the contrary, conversely,* and *on the other hand,* to move smoothly between comparison points and hold your essay together.

Because the comparative essay is a favorite of professors, especially for essay exams, it's useful to know a couple of time-honored ways to structure this type of paper.

Both common structures begin with a thesis statement (which all your comparison points will link back to) that clearly shows the relationship of the two items you are comparing and often includes the word *whereas:*

Thesis: Whereas painter Alice Neel and photographer Diane Arbus used completely different media, both women captured in their art the *zeitgeist* of the experience of mid-century American women.

Parallel-order comparison (also called a text-by-text comparison):

First similarity

First work

Second work

Second similarity

First work

Second work

First difference

First work

Second work

Second difference

First work

Second work

Conclusion that refers back to thesis statement

Point-by-point comparison:

Thesis

First point

Similarities between the two works (or components/aspects of works)

Differences between the two works

Second point

Similarities between the two works

Differences between the two works

Third point

Similarities between the two works

Differences between the two works

Conclusion that refers back to thesis statement

Study Stressors _____

Common flaws with comparative essays include unbalanced comparisons that give too much emphasis to some points while shortchanging others, conclusions that do no more than summarize what you've said in the body of the essay, and conclusions that don't really make a point because they state that the items being compared are similar yet different.

Argumentative Essays

The argumentative essay answers the question "How did you reach that conclusion?" The paper sets forth a premise and then, in sequence, takes the reader through the writer's thought process to show how the writer arrived at his or her conclusion. Your instructor seeks clear, convincing evidence that you have thought through the matter at hand.

Choose a topic that is controversial yet well defined and not too broad. It should be an issue about which you can find sufficient research.

Check newspapers, news magazines, TV news, interviews, and debate shows (such as the newsmaker shows on Sunday mornings), the nonfiction book bestseller list, and Internet news and blog sites for current and interesting topics.

To write an effective argumentative essay, you must develop expertise on the issue you're writing about, including the side of the issue that does *not* represent your view. This is a time to question your beliefs because your argumentative essay will be effective only if you've clearly researched and presented both sides. Be sure to maintain a professional, even-handed tone in your paper, not one that's vitriolic or hysterical.

Support your arguments with the following:

- Facts

- Statistics

- Analogies

- Your own experience, if appropriate

- Quotes from experts

- Interviews with those who have opinions or expertise on the issue

- Information from scholarly and popular literature

- Survey research (if you conduct survey research, make sure that it is statistically sound and your survey is well designed)

Acknowledge and address opposing arguments in your essay. Indicate underlying reasons that opponents hold their opinions. You can agree that there is some validity to the opposition's point but that those points are not strong enough to negate your argument. You can also make a case for complete disagreement with the opposing argument or state that it is irrelevant.

Writing Approaches

Various approaches are possible with argumentative essays, including induction, pros and cons, cause and effect, and analysis of alternatives.

The following shows effective ways to structure argumentative essays based on the approach you take:

Induction

Premise

Individual paragraphs, each containing a set of facts and observations related to the premise, including the history of the issue, the extent of the issue, repercussions/consequences of the issue, or arguments that address possible objections to your opinion

Conclusion that considers all the preceding facts

Pros and cons

First premise

Detailed examples of first premise

Opposing premise

Detailed examples of opposing premise

A balanced conclusion

Cause and effect

Premise/problem

First cause

Second cause

Third cause

Conclusion/solution

Analysis of alternatives

Premise/problem

First alternative

Second alternative

Third alternative

Conclusion/solution

The argumentative essay has its roots in the world of logic; thus, the more you know about such logic terms such as syllogisms premises, and valid deductions, the better you will be at argumentation. You can learn more about logic terms and their use at http://owl.english.purdue.edu/owl/resource/659/01/.

Pitfalls

Experts caution against these pitfalls with the argumentative essay:

◆ Choosing a topic that has been done to death. Not only will your professor be tired of reading another paper on abortion, gun control, or capital punishment, but he or she also will be quite familiar with all the arguments, which can put your paper in a negative light if you fail to present the arguments well.

◆ Using first person. Although an argumentative essay is your opinion, your argument will be stronger if you do not present your thesis as, for example, "I believe that we must all take action to slow the progress of global warming." Instead, simply state: "We must all take action to slow the progress of global warming."

◆ Using examples that the reader can't relate to or that are too narrow or irrelevant.

◆ Oversimplifying or generalizing too hastily, broadly, abstractly, or superficially in your conclusion.

◆ Using emotional arguments.

Research Papers

The majority of papers you will be assigned in college are research papers. The research you collect for a research paper illuminates what scholars have to say concerning the argument or research question you are setting forth. This serves as a springboard for your conclusion.

In preparing a research paper, strike a balance between showcasing thorough research and presenting research that covers too much ground or goes too far afield of your topic. It's easy to get carried away with research as you discover more interesting aspects of your topic. You will certainly want to include all the research you can find that closely relates to your topic. However, you may want to limit your coverage to the most recent works. On the other hand, be sure to include the landmark works in the field, no matter how old they are.

In some classes, professors will ask that you go beyond making a simple argument and discussing it based on what other scholars have contributed to the conversation on the subject. In social science, business, and natural science classes, for example, your instructor may ask that you conduct original research, such as a study or experiment. In those cases, you would likely structure your paper like this:

Introduction/thesis statement/hypothesis

Literature review (the scholarly conversation about your topic)

Explanation/methodology of study/experiment/original research

Results of study/experiment/original research

Discussion/suggestions for further research/limitations of original research

Conclusion, which refers back to the thesis statement

If your professor does not require original research, the structure of your paper would focus on the introduction, review, and conclusion.

With a research paper that focuses on only the research others have done (rather than original research you've produced), remember this key: whatever argument or thesis statement you've set forth, you must demonstrate that you have thoroughly researched and presented what all relevant sources have to say about the subject. This sets the stage for you to add to the body of research with your own analysis and assertions. (Refer back to Chapter 11 for key information on how to gather the research you need.)

Professors reward with good grades student essay and research-paper writers who understand their paper topic, support their thesis with solid research, organize their paper well, write clearly, and avoid the major flaws that irritate teachers.

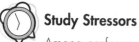

Study Stressors

> Among professors' pet peeves about research papers is little evidence of research. Inserting quotations, citing authors that bolster your thesis, and presenting a lengthy-but-pertinent bibliography will all help show your professor that you've researched your topic well (assuming that you have, in fact, gathered sufficient research material). But evidence of copious research will succeed only if you use the research you've uncovered in a way that logically supports your thesis. Integrating that research into the paper is trickier. A former colleague who is a history professor offers this stringent guideline: "Every paragraph except the introduction and conclusion ought to have a reference to the primary or secondary material used for your paper. If there is not a reference to a source in the paragraph, you probably have not provided the necessary evidence to demonstrate your point."

What You've Learned

Ready for a quick check to see what you've learned from this chapter? I now understand …

- ◆ The nuances of commonly assigned types of college papers.

- ◆ What professors are looking for in each type of paper.

- ◆ The importance of supporting my thesis statement in papers.

- ◆ How to avoid typical flaws in college papers.

- ◆ That various types of papers are building blocks for others.

The Least You Need to Know

- ◆ Most college writing outside of creative writing classes is expository, and expository writing comes in many forms.

- ◆ Virtually all expository papers contain a thesis statement or its equivalent, which must then be supported in the body of the paper and referred back to in the conclusion.

- ◆ Students who understand the basics of the most commonly assigned types of college paper will be able to build on those basics in most other types of college writing, including essay tests.

Part 5

Tackling Tough Issues

What do you do when the stress gets to be too much? How do you balance class and studying with all your other obligations? What do you do when, no matter what you do, you still receive lower grades than you expect?

Beyond all your study and test-prep efforts, succeeding in college is about managing stress and achieving balance. Here we give you lots of tips and advice for conquering stress and balancing all your commitments. Also included is a chapter on strategies for helping you through rough patches when the grades you seek are simply not happening.

Chapter 14

Managing Stress and Achieving Balance

In This Chapter

- ◆ Learn about the top stressors facing college students
- ◆ Discover stress-relief and relaxation methods
- ◆ Understand the importance of balance in your life
- ◆ Recognize the many ways to turn things down politely

Part of achieving academic success comes from having the ability to study and earn good grades—which you can't do if you are overwhelmed with stress and struggling to cope with everyday life.

For many people, college is one of the most stressful periods of their lives, partly because it's at the precipice of the major life event of transitioning from child to adult. Part of it is the college environment.

The good news to remember from this chapter is that some level of stress is actually beneficial for most of us. Stress forces us to be more efficient and effective, allowing us to actually accomplish more things—often more successfully. The problem arises, of course, when the stress keeps creeping forward and eventually becomes too much. We reach a breaking point, and things start to unravel.

This chapter is about helping you identify common college stressors, learning ways to deal with and reduce stress, recognizing the importance of having balance in your life, and providing you with ways to say "no" when you have to.

Top College Stressors

For many students, college is about growing up. College is a chance to be away from home and discover who you are and what you want from life. College is a time of major life changes and transitions, many of which cause stress.

Academic Stress

Many students are shocked at the difference between the academic demands of high school versus college. At first glance, college seems so much less demanding. Classes meet only two or three times a week, compared to daily, and there appears to be so much more free time in college than in high school. Of course, in college, students also choose whether to actually attend classes, whereas in high school, your family made sure you went to school every day.

Many high school students never learn strong—or any—study habits and arrive at college expecting that they can use the same techniques in college that helped them excel in high school. Sadly, in many situations, students learn a hard lesson the first semester that their study skills are quite deficient.

Study Stories

"I definitely made many changes in my studying habits transitioning from high school to college. In high school, all I needed to do was read over my notes real quick, and after a half-hour of 'studying,' I was ready to take the test. On top of this, I got good grades! But once I came to college, my studying habits came crashing down. It takes a while to find what method of studying works best for you."

—Tracy H.

But study skills—or a lack of them—is not the only academic stressor facing college students. Professors assign a large volume of work—readings, projects, and papers—and you need to find a way to cope with the workload. As we discuss in Chapter 4, time-management and organizational skills are essential for college students—and a very effective method of reducing the stress of the hefty workload you face.

Study Stories

"The most important thing that you need to keep in mind when going to college is that you are not in high school anymore. Hours needed for studying will be longer, assignments will be more difficult and time-consuming, and professors will expect a greater level of professionalism in reports and presentations."

—Jim B.

Personal Stress

Without question, the time spent at college is a time of great personal discovery and development. For many students, it is the first chance to live somewhat independently—at least, away from family rules and influences. Some students face some of the most fundamental questions of their lives, dealing with such issues as faith and sexual orientation. For others, college is about possibly having the first significant personal and sexual relationships.

In other words, college is about personal freedom and discovery. Students discover who they really are—and what they stand for—while in college.

That's all good and wonderful, right? Of course, major decisions and discoveries like these are major causes of stress—especially if the personal development moves you away from how you were raised by your family.

Other personal stresses involve your personal relationships with your roommates, friends, and significant others. While most personal relationships are positive, they can also greatly add to your stress level—and even have habits counter to your study habits and academic goals.

Your self-image—socially, physically, and academically—can also be a major stressor for you. Female students especially deal with stress related to weight gain and physical appearance, but all students deal with the stress of how they are perceived. And sometimes it's a vicious cycle because some people are "stress eaters"; while being stressed about their body, they actually eat to deal with the stress.

Study Stories _____

"I struggled for a bit in college with some personal demons—most of the time just wallowing in the self-pity I found as a safe haven from all the stress. While I did have some tough times academically, one of my biggest stressors—and this sounds so petty now—was how I looked, how I was perceived by people. I put on the 'freshman 15' and then some, and even after I lost the weight, controlling my eating and looks became a big thing for me—too big. I wish I had sought help from the counseling center and maybe made most of college a lot easier for me."
—Jill S.

Finally, there are the other freedom and peer pressure issues of alcohol and drug use. Most colleges report—even if unofficially—a high level of alcohol use and binge drinking by their students, including underage drinkers. Almost half of students report drinking in a high-risk manner at some point in the college career, and one in five students reports drinking in a high-risk manner often. And besides the ever-present threat of the use of illegal substances, there is also strong evidence of more students misusing, abusing, and sharing various prescription drugs.

Study Stressors _____

Some students turn to alcohol or other drugs mistakenly thinking that they're dealing with stress, when in fact these simply increase stress levels. Plus your brain simply does not function well when you abuse it with alcohol or other drugs. Don't use the excuse of a drug as a stress reducer—it will have great negative impacts personally and academically.

Family Stress

College students who live on campus do get some physical distance from their families, but they're never more than a phone call or e-mail away from a parental guilt trip—even an unintentional one.

Experts expect family stress to continue, especially with the increasing occurrence of so-called helicopter parents—those parents who are so involved in their children's lives that they are in almost constant contact.

Study Stories

"My parents, especially my dad, expected me to become either a doctor or a lawyer. He's a pharmacist, so I'm not sure why, except that he wanted a better life for me. And while I think I actually did have some interest in those fields, it's sometimes hard to tell if I ever did or if this was just because my parents talked about it so much. Anyway, I did do pre-med for a while and also joined the pre-law club, but my grades in the core courses were just not there, and the stress just became unbearable. I considered dropping out of college. I did finally talk with my parents, and while I think they are still disappointed, they have told me it's my life and I should pursue what I want to do."

—Steve B.

And college students with older (and perhaps more successful) siblings may face unrealistic expectations from their parents. First-generation college students also carry the burden of success—to be the first in the family to graduate college.

Of course, family members always mean well. But unless you take some sort of initiative to stop all the "encouragement," you will continue to face a great deal of unnecessary stress in college.

Finally, stress can also come from being away from your family and family holidays and traditions—being homesick. Cope with this stress by being active on campus and developing a new family of friends.

Financial Stress

There's no question that college costs continue to rise, placing increasing pressure on both students and their families to find a way to foot the bill.

About two thirds of college students have student loan debt, with an average $21,000 student loan debt load for graduating college seniors nationwide, according to the Project on Student Debt, an initiative of the Institute for College Access and Success, an independent, nonprofit organization trying to make college more affordable.

And while $21,000 may seem like a lot, considering that public college costs an average of about $13,000 a year and private schools costs $28,000, the debt load could certainly be much higher—and is much higher for some students.

But there are also a lot of other hidden costs related to college, such as books and school supplies, cell phones, personal-care and clothing purchases, items to decorate dorm rooms, social outings, various student clubs and organizations, and miscellaneous charges and tickets.

Besides the stress of needing the financial resources to pay all these bills, some college students work part time, either through work-study in college or with a local employer. Because working hours take away from studying hours, the need to work also causes stress.

Future Stress

It's natural for the current generation to want to be more successful than their parents, but because the baby boomers have generally been a successful group, today's college students feel even more pressure to succeed.

Some high schools are pushing students to choose career tracks, and in college, students are urged to obtain internships and other work experiences in preparation for their careers. The pressure to choose the "right" major in college is great.

An interesting outcome of this stress is a large number of students showing signs of what we call the "Peter Pan Syndrome." These students go to great lengths to avoid any kind of discussions about the future (and growing up), and college graduation is always far away in the distant future.

Stress Relief, Wellness, and Relaxation Techniques

You'll be able to study much easier, feel better about yourself, and achieve higher academic achievement when you directly deal with the stresses you face.

The first thing you should do is either find a way to remove the stress or remove yourself from the stressful situation. For example, if your roommate is stressing you out, walk away from the situation and take the time to cool down. If you can't work things out, do a roommate switch to permanently remove yourself from the situation.

The second thing you might consider is talking it out with an impartial person to get a different perspective on the situation. The situation might not be as bad as you think—or you may simply need to develop a thicker skin.

The third thing to consider is to take yourself out of it. This is especially worthwhile if the stress is related to a feeling of competition with others (over appearance, possessions, reputation, grades, or other accomplishments).

Study Suggestions

What are the best defenses against chronic, ongoing stress? Most experts suggest four methods for relieving the pressures from stress. First, consider some physical activity, such as exercise. Second, you might consider a relaxation technique, such as meditation. Third, some students find great relief from personal empowerment exercises, such as positive self-talk. Finally, always consider simply talking it out with your social network of friends and family.

Symptoms of Stress

How stressed are you? If you are regularly suffering from one or more of these stress symptoms, talk to a trusted professor or staff member, or seek the guidance of a professional from your school's counseling center:

- High levels of anxiety

- Feelings of depression

- Abuse of alcohol or drugs

- Overeating or undereating

- Difficulty making connections

- High levels of irritability, mood swings

- Constant headaches

- Too much or not enough sleep

- Lingering illnesses and aches and pains

- Urge to harm yourself

Stress Relief

The best way to immediately relieve stress is to do something physical (as long as you are physically capable of doing so). This helps release some of the pent-up energy and anxiety caused by stress. Exercising also decreases the output of stress hormones and helps you get a better sleep.

Study Stories

"I prefer something extremely cardio to relieve stress, such as kickboxing, step, spinning, Tae Bo, or dance cardio. But it can also be something soothing, such as a toning or yoga class. It gets the adrenaline moving through your body, and endorphins make you feel great and energize you."

—Adrianne W.

Here are some other simple ways to reduce stress:

- Ride your bike.

- Take a walk.

- Work on some homework.
- Go to the movies.
- Visit a museum.
- Surf the Internet.
- Play a video game.
- Draw, color, or mold clay.
- Listen to music.
- Watch a DVD or television.
- Bake something.
- Play a sport.
- Perform an act of kindness.
- Play with your pet.
- Take a nap.
- Sit under a tree.
- Talk (vent) with a friend.
- Laugh, cry, or scream.

Other ways of dealing with stress include seeking a balance and learning to say no, both of which we'll cover in the next sections of this chapter. Another way to deal with stress from overwork and procrastination is to develop a time-management system, as we discuss in Chapter 4.

Finally, remember that serious levels of stress require serious action. In these cases, seek help from professionals.

Wellness

Wellness plays a critical role in your ability to study and achieve greater academic success.

Wellness is about taking an active role in becoming aware of and making choices toward a healthy existence. While colleges do a pretty decent job with physical and emotional wellness programs, students need to be aware of four other aspects of wellness beyond physical and emotional wellness.

Wellness, as defined by Dr. Bill Hettler, co-founder of the National Wellness Institute, involves integrating the body, mind, and spirit. It includes six concepts:

- *Physical wellness* deals with a perception and expectation of physical health. This includes regular physical activities, proper nutrition, and personal hygiene.

- *Emotional wellness* involves a secure self-concept and a positive sense of self, as well as the ability to cope with unpleasant mood states. This includes being able to freely express emotions and feelings, and develop positive self-esteem.

- *Spiritual wellness* relates to having a positive perception of one's meaning and purpose in life. This involves the desire for harmony with the universe and an openness to diverse multicultural beliefs and backgrounds.

- *Intellectual wellness* is about having a strong desire to learn, grow intellectually, and seek new experiences. It involves finding creative and stimulating mental activities.

- *Social wellness* revolves around having the positive support of family and friends. This involves developing long-lasting healthy friendships, and time and energy contributed to the community in which you live.

- *Occupational wellness* relates to envisioning and planning for a healthy future. This includes finding a satisfying and rewarding major and career (and, in some cases, graduate studies).

Relaxation Techniques

Relaxation techniques, which are designed to decrease the wear and tear of stress on your mind and body, are a great way to deal with the pressures you face as a college student.

Relaxation techniques have been shown to have many benefits, including these:

◆ Fewer negative emotions, such as anger and frustration

◆ Fewer negative physical issues, such as headaches

◆ Increased energy levels

◆ Improved concentration abilities

Following are the most popular forms of mental and physical relaxation techniques. All require you to find a comfortable and quiet place to sit for at least 10 minutes. Before you start any of these, remember to breathe deeply and exhale slowly three or four times.

Autogenic relaxation: A kind of self-hypnosis in which you close your eyes and use repeated words or suggestions ("I feel good" or "I am relaxed and at peace"), along with visual imagery and body awareness, to reduce stress. Feelings of heaviness, warmth, or lightness may result and are key signs of mental relaxation.

Progressive relaxation: A technique in which you tighten and release different muscle groups one at a time, typically beginning at your head or feet and progressively working in the opposite direction. The idea behind this method is to help you focus on the difference between muscle tension and relaxation, relieving tension and stress from the muscle holding it.

Visualization: A process in which you focus on a pleasant mental picture of a safe and comfortable place, such as a cool forest, a sunny beach, a fireplace on a cold day, or a quiet park. Then you take a visual journey. The key is to enlist as many of your senses as you can so that you actually have the sensation of being in that place.

Study Suggestions

You can find both relaxation scripts and music on the web. Consider downloading some and have a friend read the script to the music. For even more fun, consider having a relaxation session with a bunch of your friends.

Music: Listening to a favorite artist is a great way to escape the stress of the moment and take time to relax. Some music has been shown to spur creativity and higher levels of thinking. Choose music that evokes pleasant memories, experiences, or people—not sad or depressing music.

Some other relaxation techniques you can try include these:

◆ Stretching

◆ Yoga

◆ Tai Chi

◆ Biofeedback

◆ Massage

◆ Meditation

◆ Hypnosis

Importance of Balance

Perhaps one of the most important things for academic success is finding a balance among all the demands college students face. Some of the best students are those who are very involved in social and professional activities on campus, but being too involved can also impact your ability to study.

But just as you can be overextended with too many activities, spending all your free time studying is not wise either. We're not trying to devalue the importance of studying, but we've found that students who are concerned about grades above all else tend to risk academic burnout.

Students who spend their time just studying in college also miss out on the college experience. College is a time to take some risks and grow into adulthood. Those who stay in their dorm rooms studying don't get to experience these other activities.

Ideally, you'll find a mix of professional and social organizations at your college that interest you. Keep in mind that you may also be working at least part time.

"Make sure you take advantage of all the opportunities your school has to offer. Don't be afraid to join clubs, take on new and exciting responsibilities, join a fraternity or sorority, go on excursions, explore the surrounding areas, etc. If you make the most out of the free time you do have, you will generally be in a better mood, thus making studying less painful. Making school the centerpiece of your schedule and structuring other activities around that will almost inevitably equate to a higher GPA, more success, and a richer, more rewarding time in college."

—Patrick B.

If you find yourself wishing for more time to get all your work done, it's a sign that your life may not be in balance. You should consider asking yourself, "What do I need time for?"

Consider your priorities. What do you truly want out of your college experience? If you could start over and eliminate all the demands for your time, what activities would you keep?

The keys to achieving balance are setting priorities and learning to say "no" (which we'll cover in the next section). Certainly, for high-achieving students, the top priority will be some combination of school, learning, and grades. What comes after academic success (work, friends, family, significant others, professional development, community) and how much time you devote to each is a personal choice you'll have to make.

Learning to Say "No"

When you get a reputation as a dependable and passionate person, more people will begin approaching you to join various organizations or take on additional responsibilities. You'll want to accept some of these situations, but for the sake of having balance, you'll want to decline others.

Declining an offer, however, is easier said than done. We simply have a hard time turning people down. We hem and haw, make excuses, and often make some modest commitment. If you have esteem or assertiveness issues, then saying "no" is even harder for you.

Remember that saying "yes" is never the right answer for something you know you don't want to do or don't have the time to do. If you're already feeling stressed, adding another commitment will not help matters.

The obvious solution when asked to do something you know you simply cannot do is to just say, "Sorry, no. I'm not able to help (or join) you," or "Thank you, but no. I simply do not have the time," or "No, I've decided I just can't do that at the moment."

If you have issues saying no face to face, ask for time to consider the offer, and then call or e-mail the person with your rejection. This method gives you the time to consider the added obligation while also giving you the opportunity to decline it in a manner in which you are comfortable.

Finally, remember to release yourself from any self-inflicted guilt or guilt from others. You are the only person looking out for yourself, and while it's nice to be in demand and popular, you need to have balance to succeed.

> **Study Stories**
>
> "There are just too many things at college you could possibly do to be able to do everything. Therefore, it is important to be able to say 'no' and not overcommit yourself."
>
> —Patrick B.

Consider these other ways to say no:

- "Sorry, but I'm simply not the right person."

- "I simply cannot take on any more responsibilities right now."

- "I'm just not that interested."

- "Sorry, but I need to focus more on my studies right now."

- "I'm afraid helping you right now will adversely affect my grades."

- "I'm not interested, but I think I might know someone perfect for what you want."

- "It's just not possible for me to do it this semester, but I might be interested next semester."

♦ "I could help out, but in some lesser capacity."

♦ "I wish I could help, but as it is, I have almost no time for myself."

What You've Learned

Ready for a quick check to see what you've learned from this chapter? I now understand ...

♦ The several types of stress college students face.

♦ Key techniques for stress relief and relaxation.

♦ The importance of having balance in my life.

♦ How to say "no" to people or groups that want my assistance.

The Least You Need to Know

♦ College students face stress from academics, personal relationships, family, financial conditions, and career ambitions.

♦ Stress overload can affect a lot more than studying and good grades, so learn how to deal with it in healthy ways.

♦ You can mentally and physically relax and reduce stress in a number of ways.

♦ Attaining good grades is sometimes a balancing act among school, social, and work demands.

Chapter 15

If the Good Grades Are Not Happening

In This Chapter

- ◆ Find ways to stay motivated to improving your grades
- ◆ Decide when it's time to return to the study basics
- ◆ Discover how tutoring can help improve your grades
- ◆ Learn the value of meeting with your professors

At some points in your academic career, the good grades you've come to expect or have been working for simply might not happen. A number of students experience this phenomenon in their first year of college as they deal with the transition from high school to college. Other students face a greater challenge in transitioning from basic college courses to upper-division (junior and senior) courses.

The thing to remember is that good grades might not always happen for you—no matter how hard you try to achieve them. In fact, sometimes the harder you try to attain good grades, the lower your grades fall.

This chapter gives you four strategies for dealing with times when your grades are not reaching the level you want. These strategies are not mutually exclusive, so feel free to use whichever combination of them makes the most sense for you.

Staying Motivated

Let's face it, you've been attending some sort of school for as long as you can remember, and maybe you're just a little tired of it. For some of you, grades may have always come easily. For others, you've had to really work hard at your studies to get the grades. Regardless of the ease of your academic successes, the many years in school sometimes bring you to a point at which you feel kind of lost and unmotivated.

> ### Study Stories
>
> "Don't be afraid to seek help when you truly need it. We don't enter college as geniuses, and we don't leave college as geniuses. We leave as learners who are determined to succeed."
>
> —Benjamin M.
>
> "Transitioning from general-education classes to upper-level classes also required changes. Many of my general-education classes were easy, and I realized that I didn't have to spend that much time studying for them. Many of the classes didn't build on other classes, so once the class was over, you didn't necessarily need to remember all that you had learned in the class. Once I started taking classes that were in my major, not only did the classes build on each other, but I knew that I wanted to retain everything that I was learning in each class. It is really important that you don't just memorize the information, but that you actually learn it."
>
> —Cayla C.

You may be asking yourself questions such as, "Do grades really matter?" or "Why am I in college (or this major)?" or "What's happened to me?" or "Can I even bring my grades back up?"

It's not unusual for students to face periods of feeling burned out on education—and burnout often accompanies a period of slipping grades.

How do you regain a positive attitude for school if you're feeling tired, frustrated, angry, or bored with your academic studies, but you know in your heart that you really want to return to a higher level of performance? You need to find a way to motivate yourself—and stay motivated.

Study Stories

"I really think the best way to stay motivated is to find *something* you connect with in the class. If a subject material bores you, try to relate it to something else that excites you. If you find something interesting about the subject matter, it will be much easier to retain information. Another way to stay motivated, particularly if you're struggling or just lack motivation in general, is to find motivation through friends. If my friends and I have big projects or tests in a week or two-week span, we'll celebrate at the end of the week by going to dinner or the mall. You can go a step farther also and say that you won't do these activities unless you achieve a certain grade."

—Jessica W.

Here are 10 things you can do to try to overcome your stress and get motivated about your studies:

1. Commiserate with your friends and classmates. While personal negative talk is not productive, sharing frustrations about a professor ("He's just so boring") or certain class assignments ("No one has ever gotten a good grade on that project") is a good way to both release the negativity and realize that you are not alone in your feelings.

2. Look for a bright spot. Even if you tend not to be an optimist, do your best to find one more bright spot for the class. The bright spots don't have to be related directly to the class; for example, perhaps one bright spot is having a week off from class for Spring Break.

"Typically, what keeps me motivated is having something else that I love to do to distract myself at times. For me, that thing is making music. Also, I try to reflect on the good things I have already and how I can only make that better, and try to downplay in my mind the importance of the grade. Then, of course, there is the always helpful to-do list which just feels so good when you check things off as finished."

—Jim B.

3. Have a talk with your academic adviser or mentor. Again, just talking it out can lift your spirits. Plus, you'll often get inspired again about your future prospects, looking well beyond this class or semester, which should help you focus on putting this slump behind you.

4. Talk with your professor(s). If you have already established a reputation for being a good student or have shown your current professors that you are a hard worker, meet with your professor(s). Say that you're in a slump but working to pull yourself out of it. You might get some excellent advice—and perhaps a bit of sympathy. (Read more tips for meeting with your professor later in this chapter.)

5. Take a step back from the situation. Sometimes we all live in the bubble of the moment, and when the present looks bad, it blocks our vision of the future. Take an afternoon off and have some fun. Go hiking or biking. Go home and play with your dog. Do something to break out of the bubble and see that there's much more to life than wallowing about a bad class or semester.

"Stay motivated! Whenever I'm feeling a little down about school— maybe it's a lower grade than I expected or dealing with a massive project that is just taking too long to complete—I splurge on myself. It might be a dinner out with the girls or an afternoon of pampering with a pedicure and manicure. Getting both physically and mentally away from school kind of recharges my batteries, and I'm good to go for a while."

—Jill S.

6. Celebrate small victories or other progress. When you think how long you've been in school, it's easy to feel a bit burned out on education. So instead of looking back, focus on the present. Mark off each week of the semester or each test or project, and have a special treat to celebrate moving ever closer to the end of the class or semester. Also consider rewarding yourself with something that makes you happy when you get a better grade on a test or assignment.

7. Break down massive projects into reasonable pieces. If you're already near burnout, it's possible to go totally over the edge when you face the prospect of a daunting semester-long project worth half your grade. Slay the monster by breaking the project into more manageable pieces and completing each task one at a time. (Note that you can then also celebrate the completion of each of the tasks—and before you know it, the project will be complete.)

8. Deal directly with personal problems. Sometimes it's not an academic issue at all that's deflating your motivation, but some personal crisis—typically related to boyfriend/girlfriend issues. If a personal issue is distracting you from your studies, find a way to deal with it directly or put it aside.

9. Face up to personal demons deflating your motivation. We all have inner doubts and fears, and in stressful situations, they tend to get stronger and louder. It's easy to use fear as an excuse to procrastinate or to never stop trying to create the perfect assignment. You've made it this far, so put those self-defeating attitudes and behaviors in a box and lock them up. If you can't do it on your own, don't hesitate to seek professional counseling.

10. Remember, you're really in it for the learning. In the end, you may hate the grades you're getting when you're in a slump, but focusing on the real reason you're in college—to learn to be a learner—and knowing in your heart that the good grades will return can be just the lift you need. Years from now, no one will ask you about your college grade point average, but the value of what you've learned will last a lifetime.

One of the ways to regain motivation and confidence is through what's called positive self-talk or self-affirmations. You can think of using one of them as a mantra to repeat to yourself several times a day. The more you say it to yourself, the more you'll believe it. Here are some suggestions:

- ◆ "I'm an excellent student."
- ◆ "I can do anything."
- ◆ "I love learning new things."
- ◆ "Nothing can stop me from achieving my goals."
- ◆ "I will work hard until I succeed."
- ◆ "I can accomplish anything I set my mind to do."

Back to Basics

Sometimes when you find yourself struggling academically, the best solution is to get back to the basics of studying. Consider taking a step back and really looking at your most recent efforts. Ask yourself these questions:

- ◆ Am I still putting in the daily hours for studying?
- ◆ Have I attended class consistently and kept up with all the assignments from each class?
- ◆ Am I putting in more time for diminishing results?
- ◆ Am I prepping the same way I always have for tests and quizzes?
- ◆ For written assignments, am I carefully following directions and writing multiple drafts?
- ◆ Am I feeling overworked or more stressed than usual?

If you honestly feel as though you have not changed at all and neither has your workload or stress level, it's time to consider going back to the basics.

We recommend reviewing Chapters 6 through 8, which are the three most important chapters concerning basic study methods. Consider new or more advanced methods for reading your textbooks, actively attending class, and studying.

In going back to the basics and recommitting to having better and smarter (not necessarily more or longer) study skills, consider taking this *Study Skills Pledge* to help empower you to greater academic success:

- I pledge to perform at my highest level at all times. I want to succeed in my studies.

- I pledge to maximize my academic strengths while overcoming my weaknesses.

- I pledge to take control of my academic career—and take responsibility for its success or failure.

- I pledge to understand my learning styles and exploit this understanding to my advantage.

- I pledge to strive for a healthy mind and body, eating well and attempting to stay healthy.

- I pledge to read and comprehend the syllabus from every class I take.

- I pledge to actively attend every class, taking good notes and participating in class activities and discussion.

- I pledge to perfect a time-management system that keeps me aware of all my upcoming assignments, tests, and projects.

- I pledge to complete all assigned readings and homework assignments—and to complete them on time instead of procrastinating.

- I pledge to find a study method that works for me and use it to study daily.

- I pledge to not wallow in my academic mistakes. Instead, I will stay positive and learn from them so I can become a better student.

◆ I pledge to use the academic resources my college has to offer me and seek assistance when I need it.

◆ I pledge to get to know—and be known by—at least some of my professors.

◆ I pledge to remember that academic success does not always equate to learning, nor does learning always result in academic success.

◆ I pledge to work hard so I can play hard, rewarding myself when I achieve academic success.

Tutoring

Many, if not all, colleges offer free or low-cost tutoring centers to students. The most common subjects that require tutoring include English (writing center), math, economics, science, and foreign languages.

Typically, the tutors are there to assist you with a variety of academic issues, including help with explaining concepts, going through homework problems, and preparing for exams. Tutors are often students who are taking more advanced classes, and they'll work with you a few hours a week to give you the added assistance you need.

Your college provides the tutors to help you tackle work in which you're struggling. Tutors are not there to do the work for you. Here are some other general expectations that tutoring centers require from students seeking help:

◆ Students must attend classes regularly to get tutoring assistance; some require proof from the professor that you're attending class.

◆ Students should come prepared with homework, class problems, drafts of papers, or other specific issues for which they need help.

◆ Students are expected to arrive on time and not skip scheduled sessions.

◆ Students should bring all pertinent class materials to tutoring sessions, including the textbook, syllabus, and class notes.

◆ Students should generally stay positive and work toward solutions instead of spending the tutoring time talking poorly of the class or professor.

Study Stories

"When you're struggling in a class, of course, going to your professor is the first thing you should do. Your professor may be better able to identify what you're struggling with, whether it's the writing style, an inability to answer multiple-choice questions, or studying techniques. And the professors will be able to give you tips based on what they have personally experienced and what they have seen students do in the past."
—Jessica W.

If you have bigger problems that go beyond specific subjects to issues like time management or concentration, your best bet is to seek guidance from your school's academic support office. Counselors in these offices help students assess and strengthen their writing and study skills by focusing on time management, reading comprehension, test strategies, and other academic concerns. The counselors can also help you find tutors for other subjects not supported by the tutoring center.

Meeting with the Professor

We've been college professors for years—and many of our friends are college professors. We can assure you that professors want to help you succeed in their classes. They want you to understand the assignments, know what to expect on exams, and solicit feedback when you don't.

Study Suggestions

Use the relationship you develop with key professors to your advantage. Professors love dependable and conscientious students, especially high performers. Use your relationship, once established, to get into closed classes, obtain job references or grad school recommendations, and acquire the best internship and job leads.

When you have general questions that the entire class might need the answer to, it's perfectly fine to ask the question in class, but anytime you have more personal issues and concerns, it's best to see the professor in his or her office. Professors have posted office hours for the benefit of *you!* We sit in our offices waiting to impart sage advice, give feedback, and offer more thorough explanations. We're there to answer your questions and provide direction for you.

Study Stressors

Don't involve your parents in dealing with your professors. If you are having problems in a class, see the professor on your own. If you don't get any kind of satisfactory answers from the meeting, take your concerns up the academic ladder—first to the professor's department chair, then to the dean or president. Involve your parents or family only as a last resort; you're an adult, so act like it.

Professors in your major (or possible major or minor) not only can provide insights into your current class, but they also can give you insight into the curriculum, careers, graduate school, and more. Some professors can become your friends and mentors. None of these things will happen unless you take the first step by visiting their office.

Not sure how to approach your professor to ask about stopping by for a visit or requesting an appointment? Here are a few suggestions:

- "Professor Hansen, I have some questions about the class and could use your guidance."

- "Professor Hansen, I'm not getting the kind of grades I would like in your class and was hoping I could come by your office and get some for suggestions for on how to improving my performance."

- "Professor Hansen, could I stop by your office to bounce around some ideas (or a rough draft) I have about the big project?"

- "Professor Hansen, do you think we could meet so you could share with me what you think are the most important strategies for mastering this material?"

- "Professor Hansen, can we meet sometime to discuss the major and possible careers?"

If you're shy or nervous—or don't want to be seen as a "professor's pet"—how do you go about overcoming your fears or anxieties of meeting with your professor? As early in the term as possible—and, certainly, as soon as you have questions or receive a poor grade—just take the plunge and decide to meet with your professor. To assist you with this decision, here are 10 tips for meeting with your professor:

Study Stories

"I think that speaking with your professors helps because, that way, they see that you are making an effort. Don't wait until the day before the next test or project is due to speak to your professor; go talk to them early. You will look better in their eyes if they see that you aren't waiting until the last minute, and you will benefit from getting whatever advice they may give you earlier."

—Cayla C.

1. Start with making the decision to meet with your professor. It's always a good idea to be known by your professors, but if you're having any sort of difficulties you *must* go and talk with the professor. Topics to discuss include homework problems or other class assignments, tests, or questions about the major or career possibilities.

2. Find the professor's office hours, often published on his or her syllabus, as well as in the academic department office. Once you've located the office hours, consider dropping in for a visit. For most professors, office hours are just that—time made available for students to drop by and visit. If the times don't work for you, or if you want to be certain to have enough time to chat, ask for an appointment; you can often do that in person, by phone, or via e-mail.

3. Prepare for the meeting. Having a short list of the items you need to clarify or that you want to discuss will help you if you are still feeling a bit intimidated or if the professor takes the discussion way off topic. Just remember to be flexible—and don't be upset with yourself if you don't get through your entire list in one visit.

Study Stories

"Attending a small school, I benefited from having professors who were very accessible outside of class. Even if you are at a huge school with hundreds of people in your classes, you should make an effort to get to know your professors, either by stopping by their office during their office hours or maybe by staying after class a few minutes to ask them a question or discuss something with them that you found interesting in the lecture. Most of them have been teaching for years and will be able to offer you invaluable advice that you will not be able to get anywhere else. They can also help with deciding what classes to take next, dealing with certain professors, and answering other general questions that you may have about the school you are attending."

—Cayla C.

4. If you make an appointment, make every effort to remember it and arrive on time. Make sure you know where the professor's office is located. If the professor is not there when you arrive, wait for a little while, in case the professor is running late from another class or meeting. (If the professor never shows, leave a note asking for a new appointment, but don't be snide about the professor missing the meeting.)

5. It's important to make a good first impression, and an easy way to do that is to actually call the professor by the name or title he or she prefers. Don't know how the professor likes to be addressed? Ask. Many professors hold a doctorate, the highest academic degree, and, as such want, to be referred to as Dr. Lastname. Others might prefer Professor Lastname. Still others might like to be called by their first names. Be careful of addressing a professor as Mr., Mrs., or Ms.

6. No matter how upset you may be with a poor grade you've received, remember to remain calm and polite. No matter how much you're struggling in the class or how unfair you think the professor is being, he or she still commands your respect because of the title "Professor." Politely ask for clarity on how you can stop struggling and improve your grades. (And whatever you do, do not

tell the professor that you must have a certain grade to retain a scholarship or play in the big game—grades are your responsibility, not the professor's.)

7. Spend time listening to what the professor is saying. It does you no good to meet the professor for advice and then spend the entire time talking, complaining, or explaining without ever listening to the professor's advice. Listen closely and even consider taking some notes; ask for clarity if you don't understand something the professor says. Don't get lost in an inner conversation with yourself. (And certainly do not answer your cell phone while in the professor's office.)

8. Always respect the professor's time. If you have been talking with the professor for a while but still have items on your list that you need to discuss, ask the professor if he or she has more time to continue the discussion or whether you should schedule another appointment. You should also watch for nonverbal signs the professor may give to signal you that he or she has to end the meeting, such as checking on the time, shuffling papers, or putting things in a briefcase.

9. Be realistic about what to expect, especially if it's your first meeting. Most professors will not give you the solutions to your problems—just more things for you to think about so that you can find the solution yourself. Be prepared to work harder after the meeting. Students get so much more out of education when they are empowered to find the solutions on their own. And don't expect an instant bond or rapport—as with any relationship, it takes time and multiple meetings to form a friendship.

10. Always thank the professor for his or her time. Showing gratitude and appreciation can go a long way to making you stand out from other students. Though they might not always seem like it, professors are people, too, and they want to be valued for their time and efforts on your behalf. Besides thanking the professor in person, consider sending a thank-you card or e-mail reiterating your appreciation for the professor's time and insights.

What You've Learned

Ready for a quick check to see what you've learned from this chapter? I now understand ...

◆ The importance of staying motivated in all my classes.

◆ That sometimes the best thing to do is get back to study basics.

◆ The value of using tutors to give me the boost I need.

◆ Why it is so important to meet with my professors.

The Least You Need to Know

◆ You should never give up on your classes—you can use several methods to try to raise your grades.

◆ Sometimes when you're struggling with grades, all it takes is to find something to motivate you to succeed.

◆ Most colleges and universities offer free tutoring services for a variety of tough courses, such as math, writing, and foreign languages.

◆ Whether you're struggling or not—although especially if you are—it's a great idea to visit with your professors.

Appendix A

Additional Study Skills Resources

No study skills book would be complete without a list of other great study skills tools that you should consider using when you have exhausted the advice from this book—or when you want to supplement it. We're not endorsing any one particular tool over another, and we have no vested interest in any of the resources we recommend.

That said, we have developed a companion website for this book in which we will continually update and add study skills features to assist you in achieving the academic success you seek. MyCollegeSuccessStory.com includes the full stories from all the students quoted in this book, along with tips and tools to help you navigate the waters of a college education.

Study Skills Software

For students who prefer a more active study skills environment, you may want to consider one or more of these study skills software:

◆ GoBinder produced by Agilix Labs, Inc.

◆ MemoryLifter produced by Learn Lift

- Recall Plus Study Software produced by Recall Plus
- StudyX produced by Jeff Computers

Study Skills/Academic Success Websites

Here are some extremely useful study skills websites, some of which go into more depth on some of the tips and suggestions we discuss in the book.

- Academic Genius: www.academicgenius.com
- AcademicTips.org: www.academictips.org
- Bibliomania: http://bibliomania.com
- BookRags.com: www.bookrags.com
- BrainMass: www.brainmass.com
- Brute Force Study Guide: www.bruteforcestudyguide.com
- CliffsNotes.com: www.cliffsnotes.com
- EducationAtlas.com: www.educationatlas.com
- Gradefix: www.gradefix.com
- How-to-Study.com: www.how-to-study.com
- MyCollegeSuccessStory.com: www.mycollegesuccessstory.com
- Smarthinking.com: www.smarthinking.com
- SparkNotes.com: www.sparknotes.com
- Study Guides & Strategies: www.studygs.net
- Study Shack: www.studystack.com
- Study Skills Blog: www.studyskillsblog.com
- StudyTips.org: www.studytips.org
- TestTakingTips.com: www.testtakingtips.com
- Tutor.com: www.tutor.com

Study Skills Books

Here are some of the other useful study skills books on the market.

Gold, Mimi. *Help for the Struggling Student: Ready-to-Use Strategies and Lessons to Build Attention, Memory, and Organizational Skills.* Hoboken, NJ: Jossey-Bass, 2003.

Green, Gordon W., Jr., Ph.D. *Getting Straight A's.* New York: Lyle Stuart, 2000.

Jacobs, Lynn F., Ph.D., and Jeremy S. Hyman. *Professors' Guide to Getting Good Grades in College.* New York: Collins, 2006.

Kennedy, David. *How to Ace Your Way Through College and Still Have a Life!* Denver: Wellness Research Publishing, 2005.

Kesselman-Turkel, Judi. *Note-Taking Made Easy.* Madison, WI: University of Wisconsin Press, 2003.

———. *Secrets to Writing Great Papers.* Madison, WI: University of Wisconsin Press, 2003.

———. *Study Smarts: How to Learn More in Less Time.* Madison, WI: University of Wisconsin Press, 2004.

Kornhauser, Arthur W. *How to Study: Suggestions for High-School and College Students.* Chicago: University of Chicago Press, 1993.

Luckie, William R., Ph.D., and Wood Smethurst. *Study Power: Study Skills to Improve Your Learning & Your Grades.* Brookline, MA: Brookline Books, 1998.

Mundsack, Allan, James Deese, and Ellin K. Deese. *How to Study.* New York: McGraw-Hill, 2002.

Newport, Cal. *How to Become a Straight-A Student: The Unconventional Strategies Real College Students Use to Score High While Studying Less.* New York: Broadway, 2006.

———. *How to Win at College: Surprising Secrets for Success from the Country's Top Students.* New York: Broadway, 2005.

Paul, Kevin. *Study Smarter, Not Harder*. Bellingham, WA: Self-Counsel Press, 2002.

Robinson, Adam. *What Smart Students Know: Maximum Grades. Optimum Learning*. Minimum Time. New York: Three Rivers Press, 1993.

Van Blerkom, Dianna L. *College Study Skills: Becoming a Strategic Learner*. Boston: Wadsworth, 2005.

Woodcock, Susan Kruger. *SOAR Study Skills*. Grand Blanc, MI: Grand Lighthouse Publishers, 2006.

Subject-Specific Software

Here are some great interactive study tool software for subjects that typically cause students trouble.

- BioTutor Excalibur: Interactive Learning
- ChemTutor Excalibur: Interactive Learning
- PhysicsTutor Excalibur: Interactive Learning
- Spell Check Anywhere: TG Enterprises
- Studyworks! Teaching Pro: Mathematics Complete by Global Software Publishing
- Studyworks! Teaching Pro: Science Complete by Global Software Publishing

Subject-Specific Websites

These websites provide some great subject-specific study skills advice and tools for subjects that typically cause students trouble.

- Chem Tutor: www.chemtutor.com
- Chemistry Lecture Notes: www.chemistrylecturenotes.com
- CollegeWriting.info: www.collegewriting.info

- Cramster: www.cramster.com

- CustomWritten.com: www.customwritten.com

- Guide to Grammar and Writing: http://grammar.ccc.commnet. edu/grammar

- Hotmath.com: http://hotmath.com

- Interactivemathtutor.com: www.interactivemathtutor.com

- The Math Forum: http://mathforum.org

- MathHelpForum: www.mathhelpforum.com

- MathNerds: www.mathnerds.com

- MathSupport.com: www.mathsupport.com

- My Chemistry Tutor: www.mychemistrytutor.com

- Overcoming Writer's Block: http://overcomingwritersblock.com

- Physics 24/7: www.physics247.com

- Physics Forum: www.physicsforums.com

- Physics-Help: http://physics-help.info

- Professor Freedman's Math Help: www.mathpower.com

- Psychology Resources: www.alleydog.com

- S.O.S. Math: www.sosmath.com

- Webgrammar: www.webgrammar.com

- The Writing Center at the University of North Carolina–Chapel Hill: www.unc.edu/depts/wcweb

- The Writing Center at the University of Richmond: http:// writing2.richmond.edu/writing/wweb.html

- The Writing Center at the University of Wisconsin–Madison: www.wisc.edu/writing

- YourDictionary: www.yourdictionary.com

Subject-Specific Books

We've included some subject-specific study skills books in case you have a need to get much greater depth for tips on how to succeed with these specific subjects.

Dornan, Edward A. *Brief English Handbook.* New York: Longman, 2006.

Manigault, Sandra. *The Book for Math Empowerment.* Stafford, VA: Godosan Publications, 1997.

O'Conner, Patricia T. *Woe Is I: The Grammarphobe's Guide to Better English in Plain English.* New York: Riverhead, 2004.

Provost, Gary. *100 Ways to Improve Your Writing.* New York: Signet, 1985.

Ross-Larson, Bruce. *Edit Yourself: A Manual for Everyone Who Works with Words.* New York: W. W. Norton, 1995.

———. *Stunning Sentences.* New York: W. W. Norton, 1999.

Schaum's Outline of College Mathematics. New York: McGraw-Hill, 2003.

Shertzer, Margaret. *The Elements of Grammar.* New York: Longman, 1996.

Strunk, William, Jr. *The Elements of Style.* Claremont, CA: Coyote Canyon Press, 2007.

Truss, Lynne. *Eats, Shoots & Leaves: The Zero Tolerance Approach to Punctuation.* New York: Gotham, 2006.

10 Tips on 10 Study Skills/Academic Success Topics

What you'll find on the following pages of this appendix are 10 pages of 10 tips on different aspects of study skills and academic success tools.

More specifically, here are the lists of tips included in this appendix:

- ◆ 10 Tips for Academically Thriving in College
- ◆ 10 Tips for Excellent Note Taking
- ◆ 10 Tips for Finding Life Balance in College
- ◆ 10 Tips for Proper Classroom Etiquette
- ◆ 10 Tips for Better Test Preparation
- ◆ 10 Tips for Working in Student Teams
- ◆ 10 Tips for Polishing Your Writing
- ◆ 10 Tips for Time Management

◆ 10 Tips for Class Presentations

◆ 10 Tips for Improving Your Grades and Achieving Academic Success

10 Tips for Academically Thriving in College

1. Know your strengths and weaknesses. One of the most important elements of success in college is truly understanding your strengths and weaknesses.

2. Establish academic goals. You should start each semester of college with certain academic goals you want to achieve—perhaps a certain grade point average, making the honor roll, or getting on the dean's list.

3. Develop a time-management system. Of all the things high-achieving college students say, the one thing repeated over and over again is the importance of managing your time.

4. Stay on top of your assignments. Even students with great time-management systems talk about the importance of keeping important dates at the top of your mind.

5. Establish a study routine. One of the best ways to improve your academic performance is to establish a study routine—a time every day that you set aside to read your textbooks, review your notes, and work on homework assignments.

6. Get to know your professors. Knowing your professors—and being known by them—is key to academic success. The more you get to know your professors on a personal level, the more ways they can help you with your current academic success—and future career success.

7. Find a study partner in each class. Your goal should be to have a "study buddy" in each of your classes. These partners can help you—and you can help them—in many different ways.

8. Take advantage of campus resources. Every college has a plethora of resources to help students succeed, and since you're paying for them with your tuition dollars, you should take advantage of whichever ones you need.

9. Schedule studying and study breaks. Another common theme among high-achieving college students is that the best studying comes not from massively long cramming sessions, but from many (daily) study sessions spread over a long period of time.

10. Work hard, play hard. College is certainly not just about going to classes, completing the work, and getting good grades. College is also about new life experiences and making the transition from teenager to adult.

10 Tips for Excellent Note Taking

1. Develop your own note-taking system. The key for you is to find—or develop—a note-taking system that works for you. Figure out what works best for you, including such elements as outlining, bulleting, and abbreviating.

2. Arrive to each class prepared. You'll be amazed at how much easier it is to take notes on a subject with which you are familiar because you completed the assigned readings *before* the lecture.

3. Sit in front of each class, away from distractions. One of the keys to taking good notes is staying focused on the speaker. If you sit with your friends, sit over by the window, or even lose focus for just a few minutes, you risk losing key bits of information.

4. Stay actively engaged, actively listening. It does you no good if you come to class prepared, sit toward the front, but quickly become disengaged once the speaker begins to talk. One of the most important elements of taking good notes is active listening.

5. Participate in class, ask/answer questions. A great tool for improving your active listening is by participating in class discussion by asking or answering questions. Another benefit for note taking is that asking questions can help you clarify something the speaker said that you did not understand.

6. Consider recording some lectures. If you have a few professors who talk extremely fast or with an accent that makes it hard to understand, you might consider recording some of the classes so you can play them back at a later time and fill in any holes in your notes.

7. Attend all classes. The best way to make certain you have excellent notes, of course, is to attend every single class. College life offers students the freedom to choose whether to attend classes or not, but if your goal is to achieve greater academic success, then it must start with attending class.

8. Focus on cues about important material. Just about all college programs have required courses, some of which might not be your favorite—and you may even feel angry about having to take a class in which you see no benefit or value. As long as you follow the professor's lecture and learn the key points, though, you'll be able to pass the course.

9. Compare your notes with a classmate. Not sure you're always getting the most important elements of your professor's lectures? Consider asking one or two classmates to share and compare notes.

10. Use visual note-taking techniques. Sometimes it just helps to see material visually rather than just in print, so consider using diagrams and pictures to help illustrate the connections among ideas, people, events, or sequences.

10 Tips for Finding Life Balance in College

1. Set realistic goals. Finding balance probably starts with setting realistic goals for yourself. If you set goals that are too high, you'll end up wearing yourself out, feeling frustrated and disappointed in yourself for not achieving your goals. If you set your goals too low, you'll have too much time on your hands and feel empty when you achieve your goals.

2. Learn to study effectively. Your education at college involves more than countless hours of studying, so learn how you best study and prepare for exams—and then adjust your schedule accordingly.

3. Learn to better manage your time and avoid procrastination. One of the biggest reasons for feeling stressed and feeling that our lives are out of balance is when the time-management beast awakens within us. Develop a system for managing and prioritizing your time.

4. Eat well. There is no question that eating a balanced diet has a positive effect on a person's well-being—and on a student's academic performance.

5. Exercise regularly. Doing some sort of physical activity provides many benefits—from stress reduction to increasing your brain's fitness. (Of course, before you jump into any kind of physical exercise program, check with your doctor first.)

6. Take charge; set priorities. Sometimes it's easier for us to allow ourselves to feel overwhelmed rather than taking charge and developing a prioritized list of things that need to get done. You need to buck the trend and take responsibility.

7. Simplify. It's human nature for just about everyone to take on too many tasks and responsibilities, to try to do too much, and to try and please too many people. Keep things simple.

8. Let things go. (Don't sweat the small stuff.) It's easier said than done, but learn to let things go once in a while. Learn to recognize the things that don't really have much impact on your life and allow yourself to let them go.

9. Explore your options; get help. One of the great things about college is that you have access to all sorts of help—you typically can turn to your professors, academic assistance and tutoring centers, health clinic, and counseling center for the assistance you need.

10. Know when it's time to quit. There comes a time when you are simply overwhelmed and there is no way out except to make some drastic changes. Talk with your academic adviser about your options—including the possibility of dropping one of your classes so you can salvage the others.

10 Tips for Proper Classroom Etiquette

1. Arrive to class on time. There are always going to be days when a previous professor keeps you late, or you wake up late, or it takes you too long to find a parking space. But the point here is to not be habitually late to class.

2. Turn off your cell phone. Unless you are expecting an important call or text, the proper thing to do is turn your cell phone completely off as soon as you enter class. If your phone does ring, make a quick apology as you send the call to voicemail—and then send a quick e-mail to your professor after class apologizing for your gaffe.

3. Do not bring food or drink to class. In many classroom buildings, food is not even allowed, so you're not only displaying poor etiquette, but actually breaking a rule. Make time outside of class to have a meal or a snack—not in class.

4. Contribute to the class discussion when appropriate. Just about all professors appreciate a strong dialogue in the classroom, but not when the comments are unwanted or inappropriate.

5. Avoid side conversations. One of the biggest pet peeves of professors and students alike is when a few students have a "private" conversation loudly enough that it's distracting to the main discussion in the classroom.

6. Addressing the professor properly. Many full-time university faculty members have a doctorate degree and have earned the right to be addressed as "Dr." Smith rather than "Mr." or "Ms." Smith. In fact, many faculty members are insulted when students do not address them properly. If you're unsure of a faculty member's status, the best solution is to address him or her as "Professor."

7. Be attentive in class. If you are going to make the effort to arrive on time and be in class, you should also make the effort to stay actively engaged in class.

8. Stay for the entire class. There may be times when you need to leave class early, but do not make a habit of doing so. If you do need to leave class early, the best solution is to alert the professor ahead of time and then discreetly leave the classroom so as not to disturb the other students.

9. Avoid signaling or sending signs that class time is up. One of our biggest pet peeves is when students attempt to signal that class is over by shutting their books loudly, unzipping and zipping their backpacks, and otherwise making noises to show that class time is complete.

10. Contact the professor when you have to miss class. When you have to miss class for legitimate reasons or when you miss class because of illness, try to contact the professor and inform him or her of your absence.

10 Tips for Better Test Preparation

1. Start early. Cramming the night before a test may have worked in high school, but this method will fail you in college. Instead, start studying intently as early as a week before the scheduled exam.

2. Dedicate time to studying. It makes no sense to start early if you don't actually use the time for studying. The best students dedicate a block of time to studying.

3. Find the ideal study atmosphere. Besides having a regular study time, it's also important to find the ideal place/atmosphere to study. Find the situation that works best for you based on your learning preferences.

4. Know what to expect on the exam. Studying for a multiple-choice exam is different than studying for an essay exam. Make sure you know the types of questions your professor uses on his or her exams. If not listed on the syllabus, ask the professor for more details.

5. Review learning objectives. Many professors discuss key learning objectives at the beginning of a new section of the course, and most textbooks also list learning objectives at the beginning of each chapter.

6. Seek clarity when uncertain. If you come across material while studying that is contradictory or confusing, raise the issue with your professor for clarity.

7. Attend review sessions. If your professor regularly holds review sessions before an exam, make all attempts to attend it—even if you are confident about the material. Review sessions are an excellent chance to ask key questions, clarify issues, and observe what the professor sees as the most important material.

8. Consider a mock exam. If you have taken the time to prepare for the exam, one final preparation method that some of the best students use is to take a practice exam a day or two before the actual exam.

9. Get a good night's sleep. One of the keys to success on exams is a rested brain. Staying up late the night before—for whatever reasons—tires the brain, and you'll quickly find your ability to retrieve information slowly diminishing.

10. Arrive early to class. Finally, the day of the exam is here. The ideal scenario is arriving to class early with all the tools you need (pens, pencils, calculators, and so on). Getting to the classroom early allows you to settle in and mentally prepare yourself for the exam.

10 Tips for Working in Student Teams

1. Choose team members wisely. In some cases, your professor will assign students to teams, but in many more cases, students will be given the option of choosing team members. Choose people who have the right skills and motivation to excel in the team assignment.

2. Get to know your team members. One of the best things any team can do to help individual members bond as a team is to share information about each other and seek out common experiences, cultures, attitudes, and so on.

3. Exchange vital information. Share all the key communications information—phone numbers, e-mail addresses, IM screen names—as well as other important pieces of data, such as class and work schedules, and the best times to meet. Create a master list and distribute it to all team members.

4. Choose/agree upon a leader. For some team projects, the professor may appoint the leader. In situations in which no team leader has been identified, take the time in an early team meeting to identify and choose a team leader (or leaders).

5. Identify each member's strengths. Depending on the context of the assignment, identify each team member's strengths. Once you have identified each other's strengths, divide the critical tasks according to abilities and interests.

6. Actively participate/complete assignments. You cannot be mad at other team members who do not complete their work (the so-called slackers of the team) if you do not actively participate and complete your own assignments.

7. Don't monopolize conversations. Even if you think you have the best ideas—or even if you are the best student in your group—do not monopolize the team meetings. The best teams are the ones in which team members bounce ideas off of each other, leading to collaborative—and often better—ideas and decisions.

8. Don't pout/retreat when your ideas are not chosen. Group projects are *always* a compromise of ideas, so you should go into these situations with the notion that even if you have a brilliant idea for the project, it might not be chosen by your teammates.

9. Monitor team progress. Sadly, almost all teams have social loafers— so-called slackers at the college level—that will not complete their tasks, or not complete them well. Request that the team leader keep the team abreast of every member's progress.

10. Use peer pressure to motivate. While the better students will often be motivated to perform their work to the best of their abilities for the grade and/or the value of the learning experience, other students may need to be motivated to complete their work—or complete it at a higher level.

10 Tips for Polishing Your Writing

1. Give yourself quality material to begin with. It's hard to polish weak writing. Bolster your revisions by writing a well-researched, well-organized, well-supported paper.

2. Give yourself plenty of time to revise. As professors, we cannot tell you how many times we've felt the warmth of a student assignment that was literally hot off the printer. A paper printed out right before class almost certainly hasn't had the careful editing and revising needed to earn a top grade.

3. Edit on screen. Read your paper on screen to catch and correct obvious errors. Hint: adjust the zoom setting in your word-processing program to more than 100 percent.

4. Spell check and grammar check. These functions of your word-processing program are far from foolproof, but they do serve as a first line of defense.

5. Print out the paper and macro-edit. Check for big-picture issues, such as organization, evidence that you understand the topic, support for your thesis, adequate research, and length. Revise based on this review.

6. Ask your instructor to critique an early draft. See if you're going in the right direction by asking your teacher to read the paper. Not all instructors will, but it can't hurt to ask. If not your instructor, enlist a teaching assistant, another instructor, or tutor in your school's writing lab to critique the paper. Revise again.

7. Set your paper aside. It really pays off not to procrastinate and to finish your assignment as early as possible. If you can set it aside for up to 10 days, you can later approach it with fresh eyes.

8. Read your paper aloud. Your ears can catch flaws your eyes can't. Listen for flow, transitions, choppiness, and confusing sentence structure. A paper that seems to lack proper pauses when spoken probably needs better punctuation. Revise.

9. Ask someone else to read it. Find someone unfamiliar with the assignment and ask if your writing makes sense. The person can note grammar issues, but the main task is a big-picture read to see how well your paper explains its topic. Revise again.

10. Conduct a final proofreading and polish. Micro-edit to scrutinize grammar, spelling, writing style, punctuation, capitalization, bibliographic style, citations, and neatness.

10 Tips for Time Management

1. Conquer procrastination. Break projects and assignments into smaller pieces so you won't be overwhelmed and procrastinate. If you commit to tackling even the smallest piece of an assignment, you may find yourself doing more.

2. Determine what to do first. After breaking an assignment into components, decide whether it's more your style to jump on the easy or hard parts first. Some people are motivated by getting the difficult parts out of the way, while others find it easier to get started if they first attack the less-challenging aspects.

3. Get a buddy. Find a friend to whom to be accountable for your time commitments. Pledge to your time-management buddy that you will complete X task by X time.

4. Stay busy. The busiest people are usually the best at managing time because they have no choice. Staying involved will force you to keep track of your time commitments while also giving you a well-rounded college life.

5. But know when to say no. Busy, involved students are the ones most often asked to take on even more. Know your limitations. Yes, stay busy, but don't overload yourself.

6. Develop a system. Whether a planner, calendar, to-do list, or personal digital assistant (PDA) device, find a system that works for you to remind you of where you need to be and when, as well as when your assignments are due. It is said that it takes 21 days to break old habits and establish new ones, so give any system you try a chance to work for you.

7. Make the most of your "unusable" time. Read assignments while commuting on public transportation and listen to audiobooks while driving. Study for tests between classes.

8. Limit time-sucking activities. Don't let yourself fall into the black hole of spending hours checking e-mail, watching TV, or sending text messages. Limit those activities to strict time blocks. Don't give up making phone calls, but do find ways to limit your conversations. One student we know makes a point of calling his parents between classes. He legitimately can end conversations by saying, "Gotta go. I'm walking into class."

9. Overestimate how long projects will take. Decide how long it will take you to complete an assignment or project and then multiply that estimate by up to threefold. That way, you'll ensure that you complete the project in plenty of time to perfect it and will be prepared for any glitches that might unexpectedly pop up.

10. Reward yourself. Motivate yourself to meet your deadlines by giving yourself small rewards when you do—a favorite treat, an evening out at your favorite nightspot, and so on.

10 Tips for Class Presentations

1. Plan an interesting, well-organized presentation. The classic structure for a presentation is to tell your audience what you plan to tell them, actually tell them, then summarize by telling them what you told them. Sprinkle stories, humor (as appropriate), and startling statistics throughout your talk.

2. Rehearse, rehearse, rehearse. Rehearsal addresses many issues that can arise during a presentation. You'll get the timing right, ensuring that your presentation is neither too long nor too short. You'll also overcome any technical glitches if you are using audiovisual equipment.

3. Carefully consider visual aids. Consider whether PowerPoint slides will really add to your presentation. Could you add impact in another way? Could you prepare slides that are mostly images with minimal text? If you decide on PowerPoint, don't get text-heavy with your slides.

4. Have your technology nailed, and have a backup plan. Be sure you know how to use the equipment in the presentation room. Have a Plan B in case of a technical glitch.

5. Conquer your nerves. A famous study showed that more people are afraid of public speaking than of dying. Channel your nervous energy before your presentation by taking a walk and taking a few deep breaths. Visualize yourself delivering a flawless presentation.

6. Don't set up negative audience expectations. Never announce to your audience that you're really nervous. Don't apologize or denigrate your presentation; as soon as you do, your audience will expect the worst.

7. Connect with your audience. Make eye contact with the entire audience, and avoid barriers to connecting with the group. Don't turn your back and read your slides. If you use notes, don't depend on them; ideally, lay your notes on the lectern and walk back occasionally to refer to them.

8. If you use a lectern, don't abuse it. Some students are just more secure with a lectern. But don't rock back and forth, sway from side to side, lean heavily on the lectern, or tap your fingers on it.

9. Avoid distracting verbal behaviors and body language. Watch "pause words"—"um," "uh," "like," and "you know." Practice and knowing your material will help. Don't fidget, chew gum, fumble with notes, put your hands in your pockets, or jingle coins or keys.

10. Dress the part. Even if business attire is not required for your presentation, you can seem more authoritative and make a good impression—on your audience and your teacher—if you dress at least to the business-casual level.

10 Tips for Improving Your Grades and Achieving Academic Success

1. Understand yourself. A big part of academic success is having the right mindset. You have to not only believe in yourself, but also know enough about yourself to know how to achieve that success.

2. Manage your courses. Many students struggle academically, not because they do not have the abilities, but because they simply do not actively manage their courses. You should be an expert on the syllabus for each of your courses.

3. Read actively. Yes, there is quite a bit of reading assigned in college. Still, part of your job as a student is to not only read all of it, but to do so actively rather than passively. Active reading means doing more than just reading, such as taking notes or highlighting key terms.

4. Utilize every class. Too obvious? This tip is not just about attending every class—though attendance is the foundation of it. Not only must you attend every class session, but you should do so with a strategy to succeed.

5. Take great notes. It's not enough to attend and be actively involved in every class—you need to also listen carefully and take detailed notes. Develop a note-taking system that works for you.

6. Study daily and differently. Every single study of academic success shows that students who commit some time every day to studying—reading, writing, reviewing, and so on—perform at a much higher level than those who study in larger chunks, and much better than those who cram.

7. Know your professor. Put another way, make sure your professor knows you. It's amazing how many students choose to be anonymous in the classroom. If you are shy or the class is too large, we suggest visiting the professor during his or her office hours.

8. Obtain the help you need. Don't wait—find the help you need as early as possible in the course, long before you begin worrying about whether the course is even salvageable or not. There are plenty of academic and personal resources on college campuses.

9. Improve your writing. Writing is the cornerstone of academic—and career—success. You most certainly should strive to improve both your writing and your vocabulary while in college. Developing better writing skills will make you feel—and sound—smarter, and lead you to greater professional success.

10. Get involved on campus. This advice might seem counter to some of the other tips in this article, but studies show that students who have some involvement in campus activities are actually better at managing their time and balancing multiple demands for their time.

Index

U–V

W

X–Y–Z